History of the Detection, Conviction,
Life and Designs of

JOHN A. MURRELL

The Great Western Land Pirate

History of the Detection, Conviction,
Life and Designs of

JOHN A. MURRELL

The Great Western Land Pirate.

TOGETHER WITH HIS SYSTEM OF VILLAINY,
AND PLAN OF EXCITING A

NEGRO REBELLION.

AND A CATALOGUE OF THE NAMES OF FOUR
HUNDRED AND FORTY-FIVE OF HIS MYSTIC CLAN,
FELLOWS AND FOLLOWERS, AND THEIR EFFORTS FOR THE
DESTRUCTION OF

MR. VIRGIL A. STEWART,

THE YOUNG MAN WHO DETECTED HIM.
TO WHICH IS ADDED A BIOGRAPHICAL SKETCH OF

MR. VIRGIL A. STEWART.

———◆◆◆◆◆——

AUGUSTUS Q. WALTON, ESQ.
Foreword by Kevin D. McCann

BRAYBREE
VINTAGE EDITION

This 2013 Edition published by
BrayBree Publishing Company LLC
P.O. Box 1204
Dickson, Tennessee 37056-1204
Visit our website at www.braybreepublishing.com

Originally published in 1835

BrayBree Vintage Edition of *History of the Detection, Conviction,
Life and Designs of John A. Murrel, the Great Western Land Pirate*
Copyright © 2013 BrayBree Publishing Company LLC
Foreword copyright © 2013 Kevin D. McCann

ISBN-13: 978-1-940127-02-6
FIRST EDITION 2013
Printed in the United States of America

BRAYBREE
Publishing

Front cover and frontspiece:
Taken from *The Life and Adventures of John A. Murrell, the
Great Western Land Pirate, with Twenty-One Spirited
Illustrative Engravings* (1847)

About the
BrayBree Vintage Edition series

BRAYBREE
VINTAGE EDITION

Many works in the public domain are available online in print and e-book versions. However most are of inferior quality, printed with generic covers irrelevant to the subject matter and little effort made to give the reader a clean, presentable book.

Each book in the BrayBree Vintage Edition series has a unique cover design relative to the subject. The pages from the original edition are reproduced in their entirety, with spelling and grammatical errors left intact. Printing errors such as faint type and missing letters and words are seemlessly corrected. Spots, blemishes, and stray marks on the original pages are cleaned. Each book includes an original foreword or other supplemental material.

Titles are chosen for the BrayBree Vintage Edition series based on their historical significance to the local and regional history of the state of Tennessee.

FOREWORD.

Virgil A. Stewart happened to be in the right place at the right time. In January 1834, the young Georgia native offered to help a friend in Madison County, Tennessee track down two missing slaves who were believed to have been stolen by a local thief named John A. Murrell. The owner, John Henning, learned that Murrell had left his home near the village of Denmark in Madison County and was headed toward Randolph in Tipton County. Stewart left in pursuit—he was supposed to be accompanied by the owner's son, but he never showed—and eventually caught up with him.

Hoping to discover the whereabouts of the slaves, Stewart engaged Murrell in conversation under the pretense of searching for a lost horse and used comaraderie and flattery over the course of their journey to eventually win Murrell's confidence. The scoundrel shared with him stories of his exploits and revealed various criminal acts he had committed, including robbery, slave stealing, and murder. He pretended to be a country preacher and as the congregation listened to his sermon, his cohorts would steal their horses. He also admitted to being the leader of a vast criminal empire with one thousand members—some of whom were well-respected men in their communities—known as the Mystic Clan of the Confederacy.

"Sir, I am the leader of a noble band of valiant and lordly banditti," Murrell declared. "I will give you our plans and strength hereafter, and will introduce you among my fellows, and give you all their names and residences before we part…" He promised to make Stewart (whom he knew only by the fictitious name of Adam Hues) "a splendid fellow" in his organization "and put you on the high road to fortune. You shall be admitted into the grand councils of our clan; for I consider you a young man of splendid abilities. Sir, these are my feelings and sentiments towards you."[1] Stewart feinted interest in joining the organization and swore allegiance to Murrell in order to learn more about its activities. Incredibly, Murrell brought Stewart—a man he had known only three days—to a secret meeting of eleven members of the Mystic Clan at their "council house" located in the Mississippi River bottoms in Arkansas.[2]

But Murrell's most shocking confession to Stewart was a plot of his own design to instigate an uprising of enslaved African Americans on Christmas night 1835 against their white masters across the South. It would serve as a diversion to enable he and his cohorts to rob on a grand scale. "I look on the American people as my common enemy," Murrell told him. "They have disgraced me, and they can do no more: my life is nothing to me, and it shall be spent as their devoted enemy."[3]

Throughout the journey, Stewart managed to write down these events and his lengthy conversations with Murrell on numbered scraps of torn paper hidden underneath his hat. He even scratched names and places with a needle onto "his boot legs, finger nails, saddle

1. Page 24
2. Page 37–38
3. Page 28

FOREWORD.

skirts, and portmanteau." Surprisingly, he managed to do so without drawing suspicion or detection from Murrell, who by his own admission had mastered the "art of learning men."[4]

Stewart used this information when Murrell was apprehended on February 9, 1834, for the theft of the two slaves. Having first escaped from jail at Brownsville, Tennessee and recaptured at Florence, Alabama less than a month later, he was brought back to Jackson and tried in Madison County circuit court in July 1834 for slave stealing and murder. Stewart was the prosecution's star witness. Murrell was found guilty of slave stealing (but not murder) and sentenced to nine years of hard labor at the Tennessee state penitentiary in Nashville.

As a result of his testimony against their chieftan, Stewart's life was threatened by Murrell's followers and one assasination attempt almost succeeded. Fearing he would die before the country knew the full story of Murrell and his diabolical intentions, he entrusted the secrets he learned to a man named Augustus Q. Walton for the purpose of making them known to all.[5] Walton compiled his notes and printed them in a small pamphlet with the weighty title of *History of the Detection, Conviction, Life and Designs of John A. Murrel, the Great Western Land Pirate, Together with His System of Villainy, and Plan for Exciting a Negro*

4. Page 37, 29. A portmanteau is a large suitcase.

5. Preface on page 3. Writing under the pseudonym of Augustus Q. Walton, Stewart claims that "I have discharged the duty and trust committed to my care by my much esteemed young friend Mr. Virgil A. Stewart; and fulfilled the promise which I made him at the time I took charge of his papers, documents and business, when it was thought he was on his dying bed with the illness produced by a wound inflicted by the hand of an assasin." *Ibid.*

Rebellion. And a Catalogue of the Names of Four Hundred and Forty-Five of His Mystic Clan, Fellows and Followers, and Their Efforts for the Destruction of Mr. Virgil A. Stewart, the Young Man Who Detected Him. To Which is Added a Biographical Sketch of Mr. Virgil A. Stewart. It would serve as a primary source for writers and historians well into the twentieth century for information on the life, crimes, and legend of Murrell, the "great Western Land Pirate."

But it was all a lie. Or at the very least, it was embellishment of the highest order.

Augustus Q. Walton was a pseudonym for either Virgil Stewart or his ghostwriter, giving a dishonest beginning to the "tell-all" pamphlet. The first edition was published in Cincinnati, Ohio in the spring of 1835, and was received with skepticism in the Tennessee press. "As a specimen of composition, it is a miserable affair," opined the *Jackson* (Tennessee) *Truth Teller* upon reading a copy.

> [B]ut the rawhead and bloody bones character of its details is well calculated to excite popular interest and give it a wide circulation. The historical part of the pamphlet is substantially the same as that given in evidence on the trial, by the witness for the state, Mr. Stewart. We entertain no doubt of the veracity and honest intentions of Mr. Stewart; but to the extraordinary disclosures made by Murrell to the witness,

and which, through "Augustus Q. Walton,
Esq.," have been communicated by him to
the public, we must oppose our scepticism.
They are too incredible in themselves to be
believed, on the mere testimony of such a
man as Murrell—especially when to their
improbability is added the fact, that they
impeach the honor and honesty of some of
our most respectable citizens.[6]

Virgil Stewart found his character and motives being
questioned. During the trial, one of Murrell's court-ap-
pointed attorneys, Milton Brown, argued that if Stewart
could deceive his client—even if it was for the right reason—what would prevent him from deceiving everyone
else in the court? Was it not likely that Stewart and Murrell knew each other, as they were practically neighbors
(five miles apart) in Denmark? Perhaps Stewart had even
been a member of Murrell's criminal gang and turned
against him. His credibility was further damaged when
he was unable to track down John Henning's two slaves
he claimed Murrell confessed to stealing using the information given by him.[7]

In the months following his encounter with Murrell,
Stewart was accused of stealing from a merchant in
present-day Grenada County, Mississippi who had entrusted his inventory to him while out of town. He later

6. *Jackson* (Tennessee) *Truth Teller*, reprinted in the *Arkansas Gazette*,
June 2, 1835.

7. James Lal Penick Jr., *The Great Western Lan Pirate: John A. Murrell in
Legend and History*. Columbia, MO: University of Missouri Press, 1981:
68–69. The two slaves were later recovered in Louisiana.

attributed the charge to his accusor, Matthew Clanton, being a member of Murrell's gang.[8]

It wasn't until the publication of his pamphlet that Stewart ever mentioned the Mystic Clan of the Confederacy, its members, and Murrell's leadership of the criminal organization. Historian James Lal Penick Jr., in his scholarly work *The Great Western Land Pirate: John A. Murrell in Legend and History*, believed Stewart embellished his accusations against Murrell as a way to deflect Clanton's theft charge against him. He sensationalized his encounter with Murrell to the point that he became more than just an ordinary thief, and Stewart became the selfless hero who exposed the nefarious plot of a criminal mastermind.[9]

The press that had initially disregarded the pamphlet for a time reconsidered in light of a slave insurrection scare in west-central Mississippi in July 1835. It seemed to validate Stewart's claims and resulted in more sales of his pamphlet. But he likely profited little from his brush with fame and the legend he created. Virgil Stewart died in Texas in 1846, perhaps killed in a fight.[10]

If not for the publication of the pamphlet, John Murrell would likely have been just another criminal mentioned in antiquated court documents. Instead, he became something more in legend than he ever was in reality. In his book *Life on the Mississippi*, Samuel L. Clemens believed Murrell to be a worse villain than Jesse James.

8. Penick, *The Great Western Land Pirate*: 99

9. *Ibid*: 99

10. Joshua D. Rothman, *Flush Times and Fever Dreams: A Story of Capitalism and Slavery in the Age of Jackson*. Athens, GA: The University of Georgia Press, 2012: 278. Penick, *The Great Western Land Pirate*: 169fn.

Murel was his equal in boldness; in pluck;
in rapacity; in cruelty, brutality, heartless-
ness, treachery, and in general and compre-
hensive vileness and shamelessness; and very
much his superior in some larger aspects.
James was a retail rascal; Murel, wholesale.
James's modest genius dreamed of no loftier
flight than the planning of raids upon cars,
coaches, and country banks; Murel project-
ed negro insurrections and the capture of
New Orleans; and furthermore, on occasion,
this Murel could go into a pulpit and edify
the congregation. What are James and his
half-dozen vulgar rascals compared with
this stately old-time criminal, with his sermons, his mediated insurrections and city-
captures, and his majestic following of ten
thousand men, sworn to do his evil will![11]

The Murrell legend was perpetuated into the twentieth century in works such as *The Outlaw Years: The History of the Land Pirates of the Natchez Trace* by Robert M.
Coates and a biography entitled *Reverend Devil: Master Criminal of the Old South* by Ross Phares. Treasure
hunters are still trying to find what they believe to be his
caches of hidden gold in Tennessee, Arkansas, Illinois,
Louisiana, and Mississippi.[12]

11. Mark Twain, *Life on the Mississippi*. Boston: James R. Osgood and
Company, 1883: 312

12. Taylor Wilson, "West Tennessee's Bad Seed." *The Jackson Sun*, June
30, 1996.

FOREWORD.

John Murrell was a horse thief, a slave stealer, and a counterfeiter. But he was not a cold-blooded killer who disembowled his victims and filled the cavities with rocks so that the corpses sank to the bottom of the river. Neither was he "the leader and master spirit" of a vast criminal organization with intentions to initiate a slave insurrection as Virgil Stewart claimed. He was really just a petty thief, and an unsuccessful one at that.

John Andrews Murrell (1806–1844) was born in Lunenburg County, Virginia, but his family settled in Williamson County, Tennessee when he was an infant. He was in trouble with the law by the age of sixteen; four years later, he was found guilty of stealing a horse and sentenced by a Davidson County court to "receive on his bare back at the public whipping post…thirty lashes; sit in the pillory two hours on Monday, two hours on Tuesday and two hours on Wednesday next; be branded on the left thumb with the letters HT; [and] be imprisoned twelve months."[13] After his release from prison in 1827, Murrell left Williamson County with his widowed mother and most of his siblings and moved to Wayne County and perhaps Tipton County before finally settling in Madison County. By 1834, he had a wife (Elizabeth Mangrum) and two children and was a farmer.[14]

While Murrell served in prison, his wife became destitute and came close to joining him there when she

13. Penick, *The Great Western Land Pirate*: 9, 14, 18–19. Penick contends that for some reason, the branding portion of Murrell's sentence was never carried out. See Id: 20.

14. *Ibid*: 25

was found gulity of petty larceny and given a ten-year sentence. But in light of her family's circumstances, the court deferred the sentence. Elizabeth Murrell later divorced her husband.

John Murrell contracted tuberculosis in the penitentiary and received an early release in 1844. Rather than return to Madison County, he settled in Pikeville in Bledsoe County, Tennessee where he worked briefly as a blacksmith, a trade he had learned in prison. He died that same year at the age of 38.

Suggested reading

The Great Western Land Pirate: John A. Murrell in Legend and History by James Lal Penick Jr. (Columbia, Missouri: University of Missouri Press, 1981).

Flush Times and Fever Dreams: A Story of Capitalism and Slavery in the Age of Jackson by Joshua D. Rothman (Athens, Georgia: The University of Georgia Press, 2012).

KEVIN D. MCCANN

HISTORY

OF THE

DETECTION, CONVICTION, LIFE AND DESIGNS

OF

JOHN A. MUREL,

THE GREAT WESTERN LAND PIRATE.

TOGETHER WITH HIS SYSTEM OF VILLAINY, AND PLAN OF EXCITING A

NEGRO REBELLION.

AND A CATALOGUE OF THE NAMES OF FOUR HUNDRED AND FORTY-FIVE OF HIS
MYSTIC CLAN, FELLOWS AND FOLLOWERS, AND THEIR
EFFORTS FOR THE DESTRUCTION OF

MR. VIRGIL A. STEWART,

THE YOUNG MAN WHO DETECTED HIM.

TO WHICH IS ADDED A BIOGRAPHICAL SKETCH OF

MR. VIRGIL A. STEWART.

BY AUGUSTUS Q. WALTON, ESQ.

RE-PUBLISHED BY GEORGE WHITE.

PRINTED AT THE JOURNAL OFFICE. ATHENS, TENNESSEE,

1835.

PREFACE.

In presenting the history of the great Western Land Pirate, John A. Murel, and his followers to the world, I have discharged the duty and trust committed to my care by my much esteemed young friend Mr. Virgil A. Stewart; and fulfilled the promise which I made him at the time I took charge of his papers, documents and business, when it was thought he was on his dying bed with the illness produced by a wound inflicted by the hand of an assassin. Even in this great extremity of pain and misery, his greatest concern was that his country should have his information on that subject. There is no country under the canopy of Heaven, which has in any other age of the world, produced so formidable a banditti, so extensive in its operations, and so scientific in its plans, as the North American Land Piracy, of which John A. Murel was the leader and master spirit, who directed its operations against community; but it was the will of Heaven that this enemy of the human family, and destroyer of the lives and happiness of man should be stopped in his fiendish and destructive career; and that he should be delivered into the iron grasp of the offended laws of his country, to satisfy the demands of bleeding justice.— The marvellous circumstances attending his detection will be highly calculated to amuse and entertain the reader, while it shows the power and protection of our Creator to those who look to him for support and defence; and may be a warning to others, who are posting the road to misery and degradation, and convince them of the final justice of their Creator, before their consciences are forever seared to his reproofs, by progressive crimes, which must eventually end in the fate of John A. Murel. If any one individual should be reclaimed, whose conscience has begun to be seared by transgression and crime, I will consider my labor more than remunerated.

It must be acknowledged that John A. Murel has never been surpassed in cold blooded murders, by any whose names have been recorded on the pages of history, and other villainous feats have never been surpassed by any who have preceded him. He may justly claim the honor of reducing villainy to an organized system, and he may as justly claim the most important station among adepts in crime and iniquity of the blackest kind. The extent of the designs of John A. Murel and his fellows are awful to reflect on. The blood, carnage, confusion and universal devastation, which were meditated by that daring and presumptuous banditti against their country and fellow beings, without the least regard for age or sex. This proves that their adamant hearts are cold to every emotion which swells in the bosom of humanity. Beings who can coolly and deliberately deprive an unoffending human being of his life, and mangle his body with as little emotion or feeling as if he was a brute—and what is still more awful to the imagination, to think of seeing whole cities wrapped in smoke and flames, and houses and human beings together swallowed up by quirling sheets of fire; and hear the desponding screams of innocent sufferers while in the agonies of death, without being moved to compassion, or deterred from their awful purposes.

As to the names given in Murel's mystic catalogue, there is no person responsible but Murel himself, he being the person who gave them as his followers.

There is a large portion of this publication given in John A. Murel's own language, some of which is quite obscene, and presumptuously profane.

There is likewise the language of Virgil A. Stewart given in many dialogues between himself and Murel; and I would further remark, that I have given the language of Mr. Stewart's own notes on many occasions.

AUGUSTUS Q. WALTON.

INTRODUCTORY REMARKS.

It has been a notorious fact, for a number of years past, that negroes and fine horses are frequently missing from the farms of planters and the citizens of the Mississippi Valley, and never again heard of by the unfortunate owners. These occurrences in many parts of the Southern and Western countries are so frequent, that they have become a matter of the greatest concern to persons whose capital is invested in property of that kind, there being no security of its safety, as they do not know on what night their farms may be robbed of a part of their most valuable horses and negroes.

The number of detections for offences of this kind, have been inconsiderable, when compared with the great number of outrages which have been committed by a mysterious banditti, whose deep laid plans and well organized system of villainy has heretofore evaded every effort of the law to bring its vicious and destroying members to justice. There have been many imaginary suppositions concerning the means which were employed by this mysterious banditti in effecting so much destruction and distress to community.

On the night of the 18th of January, 1834, Parson John Henning and his son, of Madison county, in the State of Tennessee, lost two negro men from their farm; and it appears that Providence, in the wise dispensation of his mercies to the slave-holding States, used the outrage committed on the property of Parson Henning, as a blessing to the community, in developing an organized system of villainy, and exposing a piratical clan, and detecting the leader and master spirit, who directed its operations against society. It was in the investigation of this felony, that John A. Murel, the great Western Land Pirate, and his clan were detected, and their awful deeds exposed, and their more awful plans and designs defeated.

CHAPTER I.

John A. Murel, the far-famed personage, who by reason of his distinguished acts of villainy has acquired the title of the Western Land Pirate, was born in the State of Tennessee, and at a very tender age he acquired considerable fame for his skill in the performance of feats of villainy. His notoriety in his native county had become a matter of considerable inconvenience to his designs, and so he concluded to hunt a country better adapted to his profession. He selected a home in the western district of the State of Tennessee, in Madison county; in this new country, where society was not much refined, Murel expected to enjoy the profits of his skill and ingenuity in villainy in an uninterrupted state; but a rich and fertile country, like the western district of Tennessee, held out too many inducements to the industrious and enterprising world to remain long in a state of rudeness. Wealth and fashion have superseded the rough fore-runner of the country, and the western district of Tennessee can now afford ample materials for Murel and his mystic clan to work on, which are negroes and fine horses. The infamous character which followed him from his native county, and his ravages in the adjoining neighborhood, soon taught the citizens of that vicinity to abhor and dread him. The frequent thefts which were committed in the adjoining counties and country, and the long trips and absence of Murel from home, which no person could account for, convinced community of his guilt; though by his unparalleled skill and management, he still evaded the laws of his country; and so paved the way to his acts of villainy that the law would not affect him should he be detected.

The first grand detection of Murel, that was satisfactory to the community in the vicinity of his new home, of the baseness of his character, was the case of Mr. Long, of Madison county, Tennessee. It appeared that Murel had decoyed three of Mr. Long's negro men from his possession, and had harbored them in a rough wood near his house for a considerable time. Mr. Long believed they had run away, and were harbored by some negro in the neighborhood; but at length the time was drawing nigh for Murel to remove them and convert them to his own use. One of the negroes had left some of his clothing at home which he wanted, so he emerged from his lurking place that Murel had placed him in, and ventured home for his clothing. The overseer happened to discover and took him; and extorted from this fellow where his fellow servants were, and the designs of Murel. Mr. Long gathered a company and went to the lurking wood and surrounded the negroes, having the one first taken for a pilot. The negroes told Mr. Long the time that Murel would come to feed them. Mr. Long told his slaves to ask Murel certain questions concerning his moving them, and then disposed his company around the thick wood so as to hear Murel's answers to the interrogations of the negroes. At the time the negroes had said, Murel appeared in the wood with a basket of provisions on his arm. Mr. Long, after hearing the questions answered by Murel, which he had directed his slaves to ask, give the signal for them to seize and hold him fast, which they did. When Mr. Long and his company advanced forward, Murel, with much plausibility, informed Mr. Long that he had found his black boys, and had been feeding them there so as to detain them there until he give him word where they were, but Mr. Long had heard his sentiments before in their purity. Murel was lodged in prison; but his friends enabled him to give bail, and many thought he would not appear on the day of trial, but Murel appeared. On an investigation of the law against negro harboring, it was found to be a fineable offence, and not, as was supposed by many persons, a penitentiary crime; and that it could not be brought under the penal code. Murel was fined several hundred dollars, and in case the amount could not be made out of his property, the decision of the court was, that he should become Mr. Long's slave for five years.

Murel made an appeal to the Supreme Court, and took exceptions to the constitutionality of the law against negro harboring. Every person appeared astonished that Murel had escaped the penitentiary; and on an investigation of the law he was about to come clear, and overset the law entirely against that offence. Murel and his friends appeared much elated and became quite insolent and daring. During the trial for the offence against Mr. Long's property, all good men in the vicinity appeared to take some interest in the matter, to get rid of so dangerous a character. All of these Murel singled out as victims of his vengeance. He was not in the habit of stealing in his immediate neighborhood before. He worked at a distance; but now his revengeful nature was excited against many persons in his immediate neighborhood; among this number he had enrolled the good old Parson John Henning and his son, who on the night of the 18th of January, 1831, lost two negro men from their farm in Madison county, Tennessee. Circumstances convinced them that their negroes were stolen, as soon as they were missing. The movements of Murel were watched by persons appointed for that purpose.—Parson Henning believed that if Murel was the thief, he would be likely to go where the negroes were, so soon as suspicion against him had apparently subsided. Some time had elapsed, and all search for the negroes had ceased; but there was still a strict watch over the movements of Murel. He became very impatient to be off; but was too keen, and had too many friends, not to discover that suspicion rested upon him. The Parson determined that if he went off, he would try to ascertain where he went to, if it was possible to follow his track. He thought that if he could not come up with his negroes, that he might get on the course that they were taken, so that he might follow them. The Parson's watch learned that Murel was going to start for Randolph, a little town on the Mississippi river.— Parson Henning solicited a young friend of his, who was at his house on a visit, to accompany his son on the expedition of following Murel. The Parson knew him to be of untiring perseverence, and well schooled in the disposition of man ; and possessed of an inordinate share of public spirit. The Parson insisted on remunerating him for his trouble ; but he refused pay for any services that he might render on that occasion ; but parted with the Parson under the promise to do all in his power to reclaim his property. This young man had lived in the neighborhood two years, not far from the Parson's, but had been gone from there nine months. He had seen Murel once in his life to know him ; but he was not close to him, and could not have a very correct idea of his features. The young man stayed all night at a friends house, not far from the Parson's, the night before he was to start with the Parson's son. They agreed to meet in Denmark, a little county hamlet four miles from the Parson's the next morning. The young man was prompt in his attendance, but young Henning failed to attend. He waited for him several hours, and he still failed to come. The young man became impatient and started on, believing his friend had taken sick, as he was complaining when he parted with him. He had concluded to undertake the trip by himself. He left Denmark about ten o'clock, and proceeded towards Estanauly, a little hamlet on Hatchee river, seven miles from Denmark. The weather was very cold and the road much cut up with carriages, and then hard frozen, and covered with sleet. It was bad travelling, and he got on but slow.

Both man and beast were every where housed, and nothing moving but himself. His meditations were not interrupted, on the lonely road from Denmark to Estanauly, by the appearance of a human being. The smoke that rose from a group of small cabins thinly scattered along a little island of high ground near the Hatchee river, informed him that Estanauly was near at hand. There was nothing in this scene to inspire or animate. The smoke from the cabins had settled among the heavy timber of an extensive bottom in large black columns, and seemed to wrap all nature in deep mourning. Such a scene was calculated to impress the idea, that nature was weeping over the miseries of the inhabitants of so dreary a spot. He arrived at the toll house and called the keeper to the door, and was enquiring if Murel had passed, and whether his gates could be passed in the night without his knowledge ; and while he was making his enquiries, the keeper turned round and observed, "yonder comes Murel now." The young man turned round but Murel was too near for him to reply. Murel rode up, paid his toll, and passed on without any ceremony. The young man discovered that Murel did not know him. After Murel had passed by, the young man asked the keeper if he was certain that it was Murel that passed. The keeper asserted that it was; that he knew him well. The young man paid his toll, and started after him.

CHAPTER II.

Murel had not started at the time the Parson learned he would, and the young man was astonished to find himself ahead of the man whom he thought he was following. He had passed Murel in Denmark. He had stopped at the house of one of his friends in that village; and was engaged in writing a letter to young Henning.— His friends had given him intimation that young Henning intended to follow after him. These friends were plenty, and many of them respectable, so Murel had the advantage; but no person knew that this young friend of the Parson's was going, for he did not know it himself until late in the evening, the day before he started. Murel wrote to young Henning that he had learned he charged him with taking his negroes, and if it was true he could whip him from the point of a dagger to the anchor of a ship, and made use of a variety of expressions highly charged with irony and sarcasm; and then concluded by saying that if what he had heard was false, that he wished him to receive his epistle as a friendly letter; and stated that he was going to Randolph on some private business, and desired young Henning to come and go with him, and satisfy himself that he was not on any dishonest business. This letter was immediately sent to Henning; but Murel did not wait to see whether Henning would accept of his company or not, but pushed on; in fact he did not wish his company; but this was his artifice to prevent his following. While the young man was in Denmark there was not much passing. It was extremely cold, and all were closely housed, and around the fires, so he passed out of the place without seeing Murel, and travelled just before him all the way from Denmark to Estanauly.

After Murel had passed the young man at the toll house, there was no difficulty in getting on his track. The young man followed on behind Murel a short distance; but it struck him that he would venture a trick on him, and see if he could not impose himself as a horse hunter, and travel in company with him—so he rode on and overtook him. He spoke very politely to Murel, and Murel returned the civility in equal address; but glanced a severe look of enquiry and scrutiny at him, as his head turned away. When the following dialogue ensued:

Stranger. We have disagreeable travelling, sir.

Murel. Extremely so, sir.

S. The travelling and my business correspond very much.

M. Pray sir, what can be your business, that you should compare it to travelling on such a road as this?

S. Horse hunting, sir.

M. Yes, yes, disagreeable indeed; your comparison is not a bad one. Where did your horse stray from, sir?

S. From Yallabusher river, in the Choctaw Purchase.

M. Where is he aiming for, sir?

S. I do not know; I am told that he was owned by a man in this country somewhere: but it is an uncertain business, and a cross and pile chance. [He had been requested by a friend in the Purchase to enquire for a certain nag, as he was going to Tennessee, so he made it the description.]

M. How far down will you go, sir?

S. I do not know. The roads are so very bad, and the weather so excessively cold, that I am very tired of such an uncertain business, and I am quite lonesome travelling by myself. How far down will you go on this road?

M. About eighteen miles, to the house of a friend. I am anxious to get there but it will be very late travelling in such cold weather. Sir, perhaps your horse is stolen.

S. No, I guess not: though I had much rather some good fellow had stolen him, than for him to be straying.

Here the young stranger discovered that Murel was much pleased at the expression which had just fallen, apparently inadvertently from his lips.

M. Sir, are you acquainted in this part of the country?

S. I am a stranger, sir.

M. Where are you from, sir?

S. I was born in the State of Georgia, and raised there; but I have moved to the Choctaw Nation, and have been there about nine or ten months.

M. How do you like that country, sir?

S. Very well, sir.

M. Is there much stealing going on in that country?

S. No, not much, considering we are pretty much savages and forerunners. You know how all new countries are generally first settled, sir.

M. Certainly, sir, I am well acquainted with these things.

Here the young stranger discovered that Murel became much more free and open in his manner, and that enquiring look all disappeared; for he did not know but what he was some person that would be acquainted with his character; but when he learned that the stranger was from Georgia, and that he had been in the Choctaw Nation only nine or ten months, he knew that he could know nothing of him or his character; and the young man had nothing to

2

do now but to dissemble well, to remain in Murel's company without being suspected, and Murel having said that he was going to the house of a friend, made the young stranger much more anxious to continue with him ; for he was in hopes to meet with the good old Parson's negroes at the house.

Murel and the stranger travelled on, conversing quite free, for several miles, and had changed ideas on several matters, the stranger endeavoring to learn the bent of the mind and disposition of the master spirit that he had to deal with. The conversation turned again on stealing, which was Murel's favorite subject ; a topic on which he could dwell with the utmost pleasure and satisfaction, as in the following dialogue.

Murel. This country is about to be completely overrun by a company of rogues ; and they are so strong, that nothing can be done with them. They steal from whom they please ; and if the person they take from accuses them, they jump on more of his property ; and they find that the best plan is to be friendly with them. There are two young men who moved down from Middle Tennessee to Madison county, keen shrewd fellows—The eldest brother is one of the d—dest best judges of law that there is in the United States.— He directs the operations of the banditti ; and he so paves his way to all his offences that the law cannot reach him.

Stranger. Well sir, if they have sense enough to evade the laws of their country, which are made by the wisest men of the nation, let them do it. It is no harm. It is just as honorable for them to gain property by their superior powers, as it is for a long faced hypocrite to take the advantage of the necessities of his fellow-beings. We are placed here, and we must act for ourselves, or we feel the chilling blasts of charity's cold region, and we feel worse than that, we feel the power of opulent wealth ; and the sneer of pompous show ; and, sir, what is it that constitutes character, popularity and power, in the United States ? Sir, it is property : strip a man of his property in this country, and he is a ruined man indeed—you see his friends forsake him ; and he may have been raised in the highest circles of society, yet he is neglected and treated with contempt. **Sir,** my doctrine is, let the hardest fend off.

M. You have expressed my sentiments and feelings better than what I could myself, and I am happy to fall in with company possessed of principles so congenial with my own ; I have no doubt but these two brothers are as honorable among their associates and clan as any men on earth, but perfect devils to their enemies ; they are undaunted spirits, and can seldom or never be found when they are not armed like men of war. The citizens of Madison have once attempted to arrest the eldest brother for having three of a certain Mr. Long's negroes in his possession ; and they carried near a whole captain's company for a guard, and if they had not taken a cowardly advantage of him, he would have backed them all—though he cared nothing for the charge. He knew that they could not hurt him ; but

11

they took him prisoner, and carried him before a d——d old jackass of a Squire, who neither knew nor cared for the law or his duty: and would have committed him against positive proof, and there is no doubt but Long perjured himself in endeavoring to convict him. The people thought he was good for the penitentiary, but he defied them, and told them they were all fools; that it was only a fineable offence, to make the worst of it, and he had plenty of friends to bail him. On the day of trial the house was thronged to hear the trial. He had employed the most eminent lawyer at the bar, Andrew L. Martin, and during the trial he took his lawyer one side and cursed, and told him that, d——n him, he paid him his money to work for him, and that he could not get him to work the way he wanted him. He showed Martin the law, and got him in the way, and he gave them hell. He is a flowery fellow; but he has not dived into the quirks of the law like his client. They mulcted him with a fine and costs of suit, and in case his property would not make the amount, he was to become Long's slave for five years. When the verdict was read, he winked at Long, and called him master Billy. He took an appeal to the Supreme Court; and there is no doubt of his getting rid of the whole scrape at the May term, in spite of all the prejudice that is against him. Though there has been bad consequences attending the matter, one of his strongest friends has suffered, in consequence of suspicion of being his friend. He was the deputy sheriff, and as fine a fellow as ever lived. After they found that they could do nothing with him at law, they formed a company, and advertised for all honest men to meet at a certain school house in the neighborhood, on a certain day. They met and bound themselves in certain matters; made rules and laws for the government of the company; and in this company he had some of the strongest friends, who would inform him of their movements in the shortest time. He got several guns, and made an immense quantity of catridges, and prepared his house and buildings with port-holes, ready for an engagement. On the day they published that they would be there to slick him, he had eighteen friends who came to his assistance. He disposed of them in different buildings, so as to commence a fair fire to rake the door of his dwelling; but they got a hint that it would be a dangerous undertaking, and gave it up as a bad job; and a fine thing for them, for if they had gone he would have been apt to have cut them all off, situated as he was—and the law would have protected him in the course he intended to pursue.

But all who had any thing to do with it have got d——d sick of it, and are trying to make fair weather with him. Not that they love him, but because they dread him as they do the very devil himself—and well they may, for he has swore vengeance against some, and he will comply. He is a fellow of such smooth and genteel manners, that he is very imposing; and many of the more credulous part of community, are induced to believe that he is persecuted by Long, when he only intended friendship and kindness, in catching his negroes for him. He well knows how to excite the sympathy of the human heart, and turn things to his advantage. He rarely fails to captivate the feelings of those whom he undertakes ; and what is more astonishing he has succeeded in many instances where the strongest prejudice has existed ; and where his revenge has been excited he never fails to effect either the destruction of their property or character, and frequently both. He has frequently been compelled to remove prejudices of the strongest kind, for the purpose of getting a man into his power whom he wishes to destroy. In a matter of this kind, he has never-tiring perseverence ; and many have become wise when it was too late, and sunk under the influence of his great managing powers.

There is an old Methodist preacher and his son who have had two very fine negro men stolen a short time back ; and this old Parson Henning and his son were officious in procuring counsel, and expressing their sentiments about him and his brother, and saying what the country ought to do with them, and all such stuff as this ; and I have no doubt but those two young men have got them. They live within about two miles of the old preacher, and he and his son are as feared of these two young men as if they were ravenous beasts that were turned loose in the forest ; if they were sure of finding their negroes by following them off, they would sooner loose their property than to fall into the hands of those dreaded men.

In fact they have managed with such skill, that they have become a complete terror to the country ; and when property is missing in that country, and there is any suspicions that those two young men are concerned with it, all is given up as lost : and it is considered time and money spent in vain to follow them.

S.   These two young men must be of the first order of talents and acquirements, or they could never sustain themselves among people and a community where there are such strong prejudices against them. And that elder brother whom you speak of, must be endowed with some supernatural power, or an extraordinary capacity, and practical experience ; for the erasing prejudices of a stubborn nature are considered to be the hardest change to effect in the human mind. I would warrant them to be devoted friends, and noble spirits, in the sphere in which they move, and this old preacher you speak of is no more even if he is what he pretends to be, and that you know, we can doubt as we please, or rather as it best suits our convenience. He was their enemy, and treated them as such, when they had not been hostile to him ; and they are his enemies now, for cause ; and if they are what my imagination has made them, he will have cause to repent in sackcloth and ashes for his sins. But, sir, to my doctrine, let the hardest fend off. They are enemies, and let them lock horns. What age is that wonderous man you speak of?

M.   He is about thirty I suppose, and his brother just grown up, and as smart a fellow as the elder brother, but not half the experience. I will tell you of one of his routes on a speculation a few months past, and you can judge for yourself whether he is possessed of talents or not. There was a negro man by the name of Sam, that had been sold out of the neighborhood of these two young men, to a man by the name of Eason, near Florence, Alabama. The elder brother was passing that way, on one of his scouts, and happening to see Sam, inquired of him how he liked his new home and master. "He is hell," said Sam. "Well," said he, "Sam, you know me, and you know how to leave the rascal; run away from him and get back into your old range, and all things are safe." It was not long until Sam was at his house. He harbored him until Eason advertised him as a runaway, and offered a reward for him; that was what he wanted to see. He procured a copy of the advertisement, and put it and the negro into the hands of his brother, and a fellow by the name of Forsyth, and told them to push and make hay while the sun shines. They were gone about seven weeks, and his brother returned with fourteen hundred dollars in cash, seven hundred dollars worth of ready made clothing, and a draft on Thomas Hudnel, of Madison county, State of Mississippi, for seven hundred dollars, which is as good as gold dust; though he has to sue for the draft; but the recovery is sure—for they can never get the negro, and without him they can never prove that he was Eason's negro, and he will recover the amount of the draft in spite of hell. Hudnel became suspicious that they got the negro again, and wrote on to the house which the draft was drawn on to protest it. They did not act in that matter as the elder brother, or the old fox would have done; though for young hands they made a fine drag. They did not go immediately on and draw the cash, as one of them should have done, but delayed, trying to make more sales, and delayed too long, before the draft was presented. That is twenty-eight hundred dollars he sold Eason's negro for and now has the negro in Texas, in the hands of a friend: they did not make the disposition of Sam, which they generally do with negroes on such occasions; he is too d——d fine a fellow; and I think they will make more money on him when things get a little still. Sam is keen and artful, and he is up to any thing that was ever wrapped in that much negro hide.

If Eason had got on the track and caught him, he could have done nothing with him.

S. I cannot see how he would have evaded the law in that instance.

M. It is a plain case, sir, when the law is examined by a man who understands the criminal law. In the first place the negro was a run away, and had escaped from Eason's possession: and in the second place, Eason had offered a reward for his negro to any man who would catch him. This advertisement amounts to the same, in virtue, as a power of attorney, to take his property, and act for him to a certain extent; so you see that the advertisement is a commission to take the property into possession; now if the holder of the property chooses to make a breach of the trust which the advertise-

14

ment confides in him : and instead of carrying the negro to the owner, he converts him to his own use—this is not stealing, and the
owner can only have redress in a civil action for the amount of his
property ; and as for a civil action they care nothing for that, for they
will not keep property. Their funds are deposited in a bank that
belongs to the clan. This is the way his ingenuity perplexes them.
He has sifted the criminal laws until they are no more in his hands
than an old almanac, and he dreads them no more. But what is it
that he cannot do with as many friends as he has, who are willing to
be subject to him, and his views, in all things ; there lies his power ;
his great talent in governing his clan. He is universally beloved by
his followers.

8. Such a man as that, placed in a situation to make a display of
his talents, would soon render the name and remembrance of an
Alexander, or of a Jackson, little and inconsiderable, when compared with him ; he is great from the force of his own mental powers,
and they are great, from their station in the world, in which fortune,
more than powers have placed them.

Here the young stranger, for the first time, discovered that his encomiums on the character of this marvellous elder brother, had reached the modesty of Murel ; or produced any other effect on him,
more than to stimulate his natural vanity, which is very great, and
much like his passions, ungovernable ; but when the stranger had
eclipsed so brilliant characters with him, he could not acquiesce in
the sentiment without a modest blush, and a falter in the voice, which
detected his feelings. He seemed to fall into a reverie of thought,
and there was a silence between the two mysterious friends for several minutes, which had not been the case for some time before.—
The young stranger had discovered that his vanity was his accessible
point, and he wished to learn its bounds, when he made the comparison of Alexander and Jackson.

It began to grow late in the evening, and the sun shone dimly as
it was sinking below the western horizon, and reflected a beautiful
dim light from the sleet which shielded the lofty young timber of
Poplar creek bottom ; as they entered the bottom, Murel remarked,
this is a beautiful scene, and will conduct us through the bottom, and
then there is no more bad road from here to my old friend's. As
they prssed on through the tall young Poplars that had grown up in
an old hurricane of past years, the mingled rays of light and darkness that veiled all nature, and enveloped the young stranger, and his
mysterious friend, were highly calculated to produce superstitious
notions ; and in those mysterious days which brought such events to
pass. The young stranger began to feel as though he was on en-
chanted ground, and directed by some superior power in his movements. His mind was filled with these strange phantoms ; and all
the old superstitious stories that he had heard or read in his whole
life, appeared to crowd themselves on his mind, while passing this
bottom. The old Parson's negroes began to occupy his thoughts,

and stimulated with the hope of finding them at the house of Murel's old friend ; and more stimulated with the hope of capturing one of the basest of villains, he had rode all day in the cold without ever thinking of warming. They had passed the bottom a few hundred yards when they came to an old log which was burning by the road side, and Murel proposed to stop and warm. When the young stranger attempted to walk to the fire he found himself too numb to walk without supporting himself against his beast ; but the fire revived him very much. As Murel dropped on his haunches before the fire, he observed :

"Twelve miles to my old friends ; and you my young friend are very cold indeed : I fear you are frosted ! you cannot stand it like me : I have suffered enough to kill a horse. We will warm until the queen of the night blesses us with her silver beams, which will light us to a more hospitable lodging. Did you ever travel much by moon light ?

S. Not much, sir.

M. Then you have not the same love for her silver beams as an old veteran in mysteries. I would suppose that you are too young to be of much experience in the practical part, though you are well skilled in the theory, but you will find many difficulties to surmount in the execution of plans which you have never thought of ; you will learn to suffer privations of all kinds, to the greatest extent. These privations and difficulties, when surmounted, are what constitutes the glory of an old veteran and prominent actor."

CHAPTER III.

Murel and the young stranger had enjoyed the warmth of the fire at the old log for near half an hour in conversation, and exchanging ideas and sentiments on the justification of acts of villainy, and the prospects of a course of that kind. When the moon began to make the sleet glisten on the surrounding trees, they mounted their horses and started. It was like a new scene to the young stranger, and produced a damp on his feelings which he had never before felt.— To reflect that he was then alone with one of the most desperate men in the world, who cared for neither God or devil, and knew no law but his own rapacious will. These reflections had set his whole imagination to work, and he began to reflect, and think of the danger there would be in going with Murel to where the negroes were, for they would know him ; and Murel and his friend would murder him before he could get any assistance. He had one elegant pistol, and he concluded to trust himself in the hands of Providence, and try to fight his way through. To have broken off then, under so favorable prospects of victory, would have been cowardly and unworthy, when compared with the management of the day. The justice of his cause braced his nerves, and before he had rode far he was recovered of all bad feeling, and in a high chat with his apparent unknown companion.

The young stranger was determined not to ride before, so as to give Murel the opportunity of shooting him, when he could not know it, for he could have no confidence in the smiles of so depraved a creature as Murel—so he rode just behind him.

Murel. Come, sir, ride up, the night is cold and we have far to go, and we had as well pass the time as lively as possible; come up, and I will tell you another feat of this elder brother, whom I was telling you of.

Stranger. Yes, sir, with all my heart, if it is as good as the last.

M. He is a d——d likely fellow, tall and well proportioned, and dresses rather in the Methodist order, and when he is off on his scouts directing his men how to proceed, (for he never carries off property himself, he always has men for that purpose,) he frequently makes appointments and preaches. He is well versed in the scriptures, and preaches some splendid sermons. He has frequently preached at a place, and before he commenced, pointed out some fine horse for his friend to steal; and while he was preaching and praying for them, his friend would save the horse for him. He always gives his residence some other course than the correct direction. In one of those jaunts he called at the house of one Nobs, a Methodist, on Elk river, in Middle Tennessee. Nobs had heard him preach a year before in that neighborhood, and was much taken with him as a preacher. He had given his residence in South Alabama, and had spoken a great deal of his negroes and farm; and of the perplexity he had in getting an overseer that would do his duty, and not abuse his slaves, and all such stuff as this, and brother Nobs drank it all down; supper came on, and he got them all around the table on their feet; he raised his hands in the most solemn manner, as though he was just going to open the windows of heaven, and select its richest blessings for brother Nobs, his wife, and latest posterity. He was lengthy in his supplications at the table; but when he came to use the books, and go to duty, he was eloquent; the same service was rendered next morning.

When about to start, he wanted to pay brother Nobs: but brother Nobs was almost hurt to think that he would suppose that he would charge him. "Well, brother Nobs, will you be so good as to give me change for a twenty dollar bill? I am out of change, and I dislike to offer a bill of that size for to be changed where I stay all night, for the world will say he is a preacher and does not like to pay for staying all night at a tavern—see he has presented a twenty dollar bill to be changed. This is the way of the world—and I hope God, in his mercies, will enable me to live in such a manner as never to dishonor the cause of the Gospel, or degrade the ministry."

Brother Nobs, anxious to render the preacher, and as he thought a very rich man, a favor, answered him—"yes brother, with pleas-ure." He ran to his wife and got the keys, took out his purse, and counted out seventeen dollars and fifty cents, when his change gave out. Brother Nobs was in a peck of misery. "Stay a little, I will run over to brother Parker's and borrow the balance." "Do, if you please ; and I will stay here with sister Nobs until you return."— Brother Nobs was not long gone when he returned, with as much pride of being able to accommodate his preacher as an East India Merchant would show at the arrival of a rich cargo of goods. The preacher's bill is changed and all is right.

P. Well brother Nobs, you have a fine young Jack—did you raise him ?

Br. N. He was foaled mine, and I have raised him.

P. Will you trade him, brother Nobs ?

Br. N. I raised him for that purpose; but I cannot get the worth of him in this country ; I have never been offered more than $150 for him, and he is worth $250.

P. Yes, brother Nobs, he is cheap at that price ; and if I had the money with me, I would rid you of any further trouble with him at that price.

Br. N. Well, brother, you can take him. You say that you will be at our camp-meeting : Bring the money then—that is as soon as I will need it.

P. Well, brother Nobs, I will take him—I need him very much : I want him for my own mares : I am a domestic fellow, I raise my own mules for my farm.

The trade being completed, the preacher got ready to start; all the family gathered around him to receive his parting blessing.

P. Brother Nobs, may the Lord bless you, and save you in heaven, farewell. Sister Nobs, may the grace of our Lord and Sa-viour Jesus Christ, rest and remain upon you ; farewell. May the Lord bless your little children ; farewell, my dear babies.

The preacher was soon gone from brother Nobs; but not to South Alabama ; but to the western district of Tennessee. That day and night put the preacher a long ways off, as slow as his Jack travelled ; though he was an uncommon fine travelling Jack. The preacher sold his Jack for four hundred dollars, and passed a twenty dollar counterfeit bill on brother Nobs. Poor brother Nobs can never hear of his rich young preacher since ; but I have no doubt but he is on a voyage of soul-saving ; and will visit brother Nobs when he returns.

S. It would be a source of the highest pleasure to me, to see and become acquainted with this wonderous man ; my fancy has made him a princely fellow. Perhaps I have been too extravagant in my conceptions ; but I know he must be a great man, possessed of un-rivalled mental powers.

M. That is his character, sir.

S. I do not wonder at his being a terror to his enemies, neither

3

am I astonished that he should be beloved by his clan. Such a leader should be loved and adored by his party; for talents and capacity should be honored wherever it is found. I must confess, that what I have heard of this man alone of itself, has excited my admiration; but perhaps it is because we are congenial spirits. Sir, if I live in hell, I will fight for the devil.

M. Well, sir, we are within three miles of my old friends; ride up and we will soon be there. Will you go as far down as Randolph? your horse may have got down in that region.

S. It is likely that I will, sir; and if I was not rather scarce of change, I would continue my journey over into Arkansaw, as cold as it is, as long as I am this near to it. I have heard much of that country, and I think the land and people would suit my designs and inclinations very much. The land east of the Mississippi river is nearly all entered and is very dear.

Here the young stranger was fishing for Murel's designs and intentions; as he wished to learn whether Murel intended to go any farther than to his old friends or not; and he wished to leave the impression on the mind of Murel, that he was scarce of money, as he had a considerable amount with him. He calculated that if the negroes were not at Murel's old friend's, that Murel would continue his journey; but this was a matter he had to learn without a direct question, as being too inquisitive would be very dangerous with so shrewd a fellow. He thought the best plan was to seem, as though he seemed not to seem;—and the stranger was anxious to know whether the time was at hand for him to fight or not.

M. I would be very glad if you would go over to Arkansaw with me. I am going over, and I will let you have money if you get out; and I will show you the country as long as you wish to stay. I have thousands of friends over there—it will not cost one cent, if we stay six months; and by God, I will carry you where you can bring away a d——d sight better horse than the one you are hunting—D——n the horse, let him go to hell—I will learn you a few tricks, if you will go with me. A man with as keen an eye as you, should never spend his time hunting after a d——d horse.

S. Sir, I am much obliged to you for your compliment and much more obliged to you for the kind proposition which you have made —I will determine to-morrow whether I will go or not; but I think I will go. I have no doubt but I should learn many things under so able a teacher, as I suspect you are; and I should be happy to accompany you.

M. Here is my old friend's—I am glad to see his cabin once more. Come, alight, every thing is still—we will go into the house.

The midnight visitors knocked for admittance. The old man was not gone to bed: but all was still as death: they entered the house, and were received very friendly; but the young stranger's eyes flew round to catch a glimpse of the good old Parson's negroes; but he was disappointed, for they were not there. The young stranger being very much fatigued, he got a bed, as soon as he was warm, and went to rest; and left Murel and his old friend conversing. The young stranger's mind could not rest in this marvellous situation, for he did not know but the negroes were in some other building on the place; but at length he dropped into a sound slumber. Thus ended the stranger's first day's pilgrimage with the great Western Land Pirate.

CHARTER IV.

The young stranger was out of bed very early the next morning, and as soon as he could see, he was looking for the old Parson's negroes; but he could see nothing of them. Murel rose very early, and had the horses caught and saddled, ready for a start by clear day light. The young stranger was very particular in inquiring after a stray horse, of Murel's old friend, while in the presence of Murel. They mounted their horses and proceeded towards Wesley, a village in Haywood county, State of Tennessee, six miles from their late landlord's. After they started, and rode a short distance, Murel remarked to the stranger:

M. Well, my young friend, I believe I have not been so inquisitive as to learn your name, as yet, we have been so engaged in other conversation.

S. No, sir, we have been quite engaged since our short acquaintance; I seldom ever have a name, though you may call me Adam Hues at present.

The young stranger did not give his real name, as he was fearful that his name would remind Murel of him, should he ever have noticed him in company at any place of public gathering; this he did not know; and he thought the best plan was to be cautious; this deception subjected him to many difficulties afterwards, as he had to pass some of his acquaintances on the way.

M. Well, Mr. Hues, what say you of the trip to Arkansaw this morning?

Hues. I have not fairly determined on that matter, though I think I will go.

M. Go, yes, d—n it you must go, and I will make a man of you.

H. That is what I want, sir.

M. There is some of the handsomest girls over there you ever saw. I am in town when I am there.

H. Nothing to object to, sir; I am quite partial to handsome ladies.

M. Oh! well, go with me to Arkansaw, and d—n me if I do

not put you right in town, and they are as plump as ever come over, sir.

H. I think I will go, sir; I will determine down about Wesley, which your old friend says is five or six miles.

M. D———d if we cannot strike a breeze worth telling over there.

H. I do not doubt it, sir.

M. I will tell you a story, about another feat of this elder brother. His younger brother was living in Tipton county, below here, and he was down to see him—and while he was in the neighborhood, he decoyed off a negro man from his master, and appointed a place where to meet him, but instead of going himself, he sent a friend.— His friend conveyed him to the Mississippi river, where there was a skiff to receive them; his friend conducted the boy to Natchez in the skiff, and lodged him in the care of a second friend.

He took a passage on a Steam Boat for Natchez, after he had lurked behind until he could learn all their movements; after he reached Natchez, he took his negro and went on another Steam Boat, dressed like a lord, and had as much the appearance of a gentleman, as any man on board the Boat. He had taken a passage to New Orleans; but d—n it, misfortunes will happen every once and a while. There was a d———d fellow aboard the boat who knew him well; and this d———d rascal went to the Captain and told him that the negro which the fellow had, was stolen; and that the fellow was a notorious negro thief—and that he had better take the black boy into custody, and carry him back, and that he would be very apt to find his owner's advertisements, as he went back up the country. The Captain, a d———d old villain, in hopes of getting a reward, and the services of the negro for some time, concluded to do so. The negro was not suffered to see his master; but he had been drilled to his business before. So the fellow waited until the boat reached New Orleans; and while the boat was landing, he made his escape on the guards of another boat. He went in search of his friends, in that part of the country, who were plenty, and made all of his arrangements; and sent a friend to learn when the Captain would leave the port; so he goes to the Mayor of the city, and gets a process against the body of the Captain, for unlawfully detaining his property from his possession. The guard took him, just as he was preparing to start his boat, and him and the negro were both taken before the Mayor. He charged the Captain with having detained his property from his possession by violence and force of arms; and produced a bill of sale for the negro, purporting to have been given in Tipton county, State of Tennessee, and brought in a witness, (one of his friends,) who swore that he was present when the negro was purchased, and saw him delivered to the plaintiff.— The Mayor asked the Captain the cause of his detaining the negro from his master.

Captain. Why, why, I, I, was told that this man was a negro thief, sir.

Mayor. Have you any evidence?

C. Why—I don't know where the man is who told me. He is gone, sir.

M. What was you going to do with his negro?

C. Why—I, I, was going to keep him, sir.

M. Keep him?

C. Yes, sir, I'd keep him safe.

M. Yes, sir, I will keep you safe a while.

The negro was delivered to the plaintiff and the Captain nicked with a heavy fine, and imprisoned; and his d——d pretty friend, who knew so much, soon had a nurse that attended to his case, day and night, until he found his way to the bottom of the Mississippi river, and his guts made into fish bait. This was the way he fixed these two d——d villains, for their smartness in matters that did not concern them. He waited until the Captain was just ready to start; and by his never coming about, the Captain thought he had made his escape, and that he was proud to get a chance to run, so he had no chance to make any defence, and New Orleans is a minute place.

He sold his negro in New Orleans for eight hundred dollars; and in a few nights he stole him again, and got a friend to conduct him up the country to a friend's house in one of the upper parishes.— Here he became a Methodist preacher, and preached like hell for a neighborhood of Methodists. He had got two d——d fine geldings near New Orleans, and his friend rode one and his negro the other; while he was preaching and praying for the Methodists, he told them that he had been down to the lower country, to sell his slaves; that he had become rather conscientious on the subject of slavery, but that the boy he had with him appeared to be so much opposed to being sold, that he had concluded to carry him back home again; but the negro was up to this, and he began to pretend to love one of Hiccombatan's negro women, and he began to beg massa Hiccombatan to buy him. Brother Hiccombatan purchased his preacher's negro, and the preacher started home to Kentucky, an assumed residence. Brother Hiccombatan gave him seven hundred dollars for his boy. He had a friend to convey the boy across the Mississippi river, near the mouth of the Arkansaw river, where he was to meet him at the house of a friend. Brother Hiccombatan is greatly distressed: his boy is gone, who was sold for loving his negro woman; and his preacher gone with his money. He stove about in every direction like a mad bull; but all was in vain, his negro was gone. The preacher was prompt to attend at the house of his appointed friend, where he met his companion with the negro. He sold him the third time on Arkansaw river for five hundred dollars; and then stole him and delivered him into the hands of his friend, who conducted him to a swamp, and veiled the tragic scene, and got the last gleanings and sacred pledge of secrecy; as a game of that kind will

not do unless it ends in a mystery to all but the fraternity. He sold
that negro for two thousand dollars, and then put him forever out of
the reach of all pursuers ; and they can never graze him, unless they
can find the negro ; and that they cannot do, for his carcass has fed
many a tortois and cat fish before this time, and the frogs have sung
this many a long day to the silent repose of his skeleton ; and his
remembrance is recorded in the book of mysteries. Thus ended
the history of the Tipton boy, and brother Hiccombatan's parson,
who vanished like a spirit, to the land of mystics.

H. Wonderful and strange man, who can tell the worth of such
a noble leader ; he is great and wise in all things.

M. That is his character, sir. Well, sir, we are within a half
mile of Wesley, and we will have a warm when we get there.

H. Yes sir, we need it very much, and we will have some good
brandy and something to eat at the tavern.

M. We will get the brandy, but I have lots of provisions in my
portmanteau.

Here Hues began to plan how to pass through Wesley, without being detected by Murel, for he had three acquaintances in that place,
whom he knew would speak to him, at any distance they could see
him ; and that would divulge his proper name—and appear suspicious to Murel, for Murel believed him in a country where he knew
no person ; and in all probability, one of them would begin to enquire about his friends in Madison county, who lived within five
miles of Murel's house, which would have upset the whole matter in
one moment, for it would have explained all things to the ready and
quick understanding of Murel. He laid his plans as follows : He
concluded to use his assumed character of horse hunter, in this difficulty, and endeavor to see them while by himself, (from Murel,) if
possible ; and apprize them of his business and plan : so when they
come in sight of the village, Hues handed Murel a flask and told
him that as he was acquainted in the place that he must get the
liquor ; and that he would stop at some store, and write a few advertisements for his horse—as he had concluded to go to Arkansaw
with him—and that the horse might be heard of by the time they returned.

H. Is that sign the tavern, sir ?

M. Yes, sir, that is the Wesley Inn. We can warm there, and
I expect you can do your writing there. I will see the fire the first
thing I do. Do your writing quick, and come on to the tavern.

This suited Hues very well, for two of his acquaintances were at
the tavern, and he stopped opposite the first store house they came
to, and while Murel was at the tavern, Hues went to the grocery to
see his other friend who kept the only liquor in the place, but his
friend was not at home—so he apprehended no fears from him, unless he should meet him coming in, as they were leaving the place.
Hues fell back behind some palings, and watched the door of the
tavern, until he saw Murel leave the tavern, and go to the grocery for

the liquor. He then walked on to the tavern, and took Col. Bailus into a back room, and apprized him of his designs. The Col. passed him as a stranger while in the presence of Murel; though while they were in the back room, the Col. loaned Hues an elegant pistol, to defend himself against any violent attack from Murel and his clan, provided he should come up with the Parson's negroes. Murel came in with his liquor and gave his friend Hues a dram, and insisted on their starting. Hues was prepared to be off, and they mounted their horses, and directed their course for Randolph. They had rode a mile from Wesley, when Murel observed to Hues—"Come Hues, we will ride out from the road, and eat some cold victuals and take a little more of the God bless us." Murel turned from the road and Hues followed after him; after Hues had gone after him fifty yards into the woods, he asked Murel why he was going so far from the road. Murel replied, that the d——d old Methodist whom he had been telling him of, knowing him to be a particular friend of these two young men, he should not be surprised, if young Henning was to follow him; and if he did, that he would rather have Henning before than behind him; if he was d——d fool enough to try it: as he would know better how to manage him. Murel continued on about one hundred yards, and stopped by the side of an old log, and hitched his horse, and then opened his provisions and spread them on the log, and set the flask by them: and invited Hues to help himself to what he could find on the rough table before him. They both took another good horn from the flask, and commenced hiding bread and bacon ham.

M. Well Hues, I will be d——d if I can't put you in better business than trading with the Indians.

H. I have no doubt of that, sir.

M. Did you ever hear of those devils, Murels, up in Madison county, in this State?

H. I am an entire stranger to them, sir.

M. I am that elder brother whom I have been telling you of.

H. Is it possible I have the pleasure of standing before the illustrious personage, of whom I have heard so many noble feats, and whose dexterity and skill in performance are unrivalled by any the world has ever produced before him; is it a dream or is it reality? I scarce can believe that it is a man in real life who stands before me! My imagination would fancy, and make you the genius of some master spirit of ancient days, who is sent as a guide, to protect and defend me, before all which may oppose. Sir, under the protection of so able a guide, and proprietor, I have nothing to fear; but look back to the hour of our meeting, as the fortunate era, when my importance and victories were to commence.

M. Sir, I pledge you my head that I will give you all the instruction which my long experience will enable me to give you; and I flatter myself that I shall never be ashamed of the progress of so very intelligent a pupil. Sir, I am the leader of a noble band of valiant and lordly banditti; I will give you our plans and strength hereafter, and will introduce you among my fellows, and give you all their names and residences before we part; but we must not be parted longer than you can arrange your business; and I will make you a splendid fellow, and put you on the high road to fortune.

You shall be admitted into the grand councils of our clan; for I consider you a young man of splendid abilities. Sir, these are my feelings and sentiments towards you.

Hues and his experienced preceptor had no sooner finished their repast at the old log, than they mounted their horses and set out on their journey for Arkansaw. Murel now informed his friend Hues, that they would leave the public road, and travel a by-way which he was well acquainted with; and by that means, if the old Parson should have any person following after him, they would loose his track: as he was going to where he had sent the Parson's negroes by a friend, and that he was very anxious to get there, as the time was past by several days that he was to have met them; but owing to the suspicions of the old Parson, he had delayed time: and that his friend would not understand the matter and become alarmed; and he insisted on travelling all the ensuing night.

Murel now commences to tell how he had managed to prevent young Henning from following him, and repeated over the letter which he had sent him from Denmark, desiring Henning to accompany him to Randolph. Murel raised his hand and swore, that he could take young Henning with him, and sell every negro he had, and that he might stand by his side all the time, and know nothing about it when he was done and had received his money; and said he had never intended to disturb his close neighbors until they commenced their sharp shooting at him. "But now d—n them, they may look out for breakers, for I have commenced my operations on them, and when I quit them they will not be quite so consequential as they now are. Their long prayers and Methodist coats will not save them from my sworn vengeance, neither will they bring back their negroes when they once get into my clutches." Hues sanctioned all that Murel said, and contended, that he was justifiable in all the injury which he could do them. Hues studied to represent himself as congenial to Murel's disposition as he possibly could, in every thing that was advanced by him.

The conversation turned on their future prospects of gain, and the proficiency of Murel, in the execution of his plans; and Murel to satisfy his young pupil, that he was not misrepresenting his powers in villainy, proposed to Hues, that he would decoy the first negro they met on the way; and make him agree to leave his master, and go with him. Hues anxious to see by what means he was so successful in his attempts, desired him to do so. They had not travelled more than six miles from the place where they had stopped to eat, when they saw an old negro at a crib by the road side, preparing to go to mill with a sack of corn: his master had moved his buildings near a half mile from the road, and had left his crib standing at the old situation. The old man was alone, and Murel thus accosted him.

Murel. "Well, old man, you must have a d——d hard master, or he would not send you to mill this cold day.

Negro. Yes, maser, all on um hard in dis country.

M. Why do you stay with the d——d villain, then? when he treats you like a d——d dog?

N. I can't help um, maser.

M. Would you help it if you could?

N. O! yes, maser, dat I would.

M· What is your name old man?

N. My name Clitto, maser.

M. Well, Clitto, would you like to be free and have plenty of money to buy land and horses, and every thing you want?

C. O! yes, maser, dat Clitto do so want em.

M. If I will steal you, and carry you off, and sell you four or five times: and give you half of the money, and then leave you in a free State, will you go?

C. O! yes maser; Clitto go quick.

M. Well, Clitto, don't you want a dram, taking out his flask of liquor, and offering it to Clitto.

C. Thankey, maser, arter you.

M. Oh! no, Clitto, after you, (Clitto drinks, and then Murel after him.)

M. Well, Clitto, have you no boys that you would like to see free?

C. O! yes, maser.

M. Now, Clitto, if you was to hear a pistol fire at the head of the lane some night, do you think you will be sure to come to me, and bring three or four boys with you?

C. O! yes, maser, Clitto come dis night.

M. I am in a hurry now, Clitto, and cannot carry you off at this time; but you have the boys ready, and you shall not be with your d——d old task master much longer, to be cuffed about like a dog. I am a great friend to black people. I have carried off a great many, and they are doing well, all got homes of their own; and making property; you look out, and when you hear the pistol fire, come with the boys, and I will have horses ready to push you. Good by, Clitto, until I see you again."

Thus ended the dialogue between Murel and Clitto. Hues enjoyed the scene very much, and was much astonished at the success of Murel, in his persuasions, and base address in villainy.

Hues applauded the splendid success of his preceptor, and expressed the greatest astonishment, at seeing him victorious in so short time:—to which Murel replied, that "fifteen minutes are all I want to decoy the best of negroes from the best of masters."

Murel and Hues had exchanged ideas and sentiments on many

matters; but Murel had yet to open the splendor of his schemes to his young companion; and he appeared to have an itching to see what effect it would have. After they had spent the greater part of the second day, Murel commenced the grand disclosure of his plans, purposes, and designs, as follows.

Murel. "Hues I will tell you a secret that belongs to my clan, which is of more importance than stealing negroes, a shorter way to an overgrown fortune, and it is not far ahead. The movements of my clan have been as brisk as could have been expected, in that matter; things are moving on smooth and easy. But this is a matter that is known only by a few of our leading characters. The first class keeps all their designs, and the extent of their plans, to themselves. For this reason, all who would be willing to join us, are not capable of managing our designs; and there would be danger of their making disclosures which would lead to the destruction of our designs, before they are perfected. This class is what we call the grand council.

The second class are those whom we trust with nothing only that which they are immediately concerned with. We have them to do what we are not willing to do ourselves. They always stand between us and danger. For a few dollars we can get them to run a negro or a fine horse to some place where we can go and take possession of it without any danger; and there is no danger in this fellow then; for he has become the offender, and of course, he is bound to secrecy. This class is what we term the strikers. We have about four hundred of the grand council, and near six hundred and fifty strikers. This is our strength as near as I can guess. I will give you a list of their names as I promised, before we part.

The grand object that we have in contemplation, is to excite a rebellion among the negroes, throughout the slave-holding States.— Our plan is to manage so as to have it commence every where at the same hour. We have set on the 25th of December, 1835, for the time to commence our operations. We design having our companies so stationed over the country, in the vicinity of the banks and the large cities, that when the negroes commence their carnage and slaughter, we will have detachments to fire the towns, and rob the banks, while all is confusion and dismay. The rebellion taking place every where at the same time, every part of the country will be engaged in its own defence; and one part of the country can afford no relief to another, until many places will be entirely overrun by the negroes, and our pockets replenished from the banks, and the desks of rich merchant's houses. It is true that in many places, in slave-holding States, the negro population is not strong, and would be easily overpowered, but back them with a few resolute leaders from our clan, and they will murder thousands, and huddle the remainder into large bodies, of stationary defence, for their own preservation; and then, in many other places, the black population is much the strongest, and under a leader, would overrun the country before any steps could be taken to suppress them, if it is managed by a proper leader.

Hues. I cannot see how the matter is let to the negroes, without endangering the scheme by a disclosure ; as all the negroes are not disposed to see their masters murdered.

Murel. That is very easy done, we work on the proper materials, we do not go to every negro we see, and tell him that the negroes intend to rebel on the night of the 25th of December, 1835.— We find the most vicious and wicked disposed ones, on large farms : and poison their minds by telling them how they are mistreated, and that they are entitled to their freedom as much as their masters, and that all the wealth of the country is the proceeds of the black people's labor ; we remind them of the pomp and splendor of their masters, and then refer them to their own degraded situation, and tell them that it is power and tyranny which rivets their chains of bondage, and not because they are an inferior race of people. We tell them that all Europe has abandoned slavery, and that the West Indies are all free ; and that they got their freedom by rebelling a few times and slaughtering the whites, and convince them, that if they will follow the example of the West India negroes, that they will obtain their liberty, and become as much respected as if they were white, and that they can marry white women when they are all put on a level. In addition to this, get them to believe, that the most of people are in favor of their being free, and that the free States, in the United States, would not interfere with the negroes, if they were to butcher every white man in the slave-holding States.

When we are convinced that we have found a blood thirsty devil, we swear him to secrecy, and disclose to him the secret ; and convince him that every other State, and section of country where there are any negroes, intend to rebel and slay all the whites they can on the night of the 25th of December, 1835 ; and assure him that there are thousands of white men engaged in trying to free them, who will die by their sides in battle. We have a long ceremony for the oath, which is administered in the presence of a terrific picture, painted for the purpose, representing the monster who is to deal with him should he prove unfaithful in the engagement he has entered into. This picture is highly calculated to make a negro true to his trust, for they are disposed to be superstitious at best. After we swear him, we then instruct him how to proceed : Which is as follows : he is to convince his fellow slaves of the injustice of their being held in bondage ; and learn the feelings of all he can on the subject of a rebellion, by telling them how successful the West India negroes have been, in gaining their freedom by frequent rebellions.

The plan is, to have the negroes harrowed up against the whites, and their minds alive to the idea of being free : and let none but such as we can trust, know the intention and time of the rebellion, until the night it is to commence—when our black emissaries are to have gatherings of their fellow slaves, and unite all in their reach, to

attend, with a promise of plenty to drink, which will always call negroes together. Our emissaries will be furnished with money to
procure spirits, to give them a few drams; when our emissaries
will open their secret as follows: "Fellow slaves, this is the night
that we are to obtain our liberty. All the negroes in America rebel
this night and murder the whites. We have been long subject to the
whips of our tyrants; and many of our backs wear the scars; but
the time has arrived when we can be revenged.

There are many good white men who are helping us to gain our
liberty. All of you that refuse to fight will be put to death; so
come on my brave fellows, we will be free or die." We will have
our men, whom we intend for leaders, ready to head these companies, and encourage the negroes, should they appear backward.—
Thus you see, that they will be forced to engage, under the belief,
that the negroes have rebelled every where else, as in their own
neighborhood, and by those means every gathering or assemblage of
negroes will be pushed forward even contrary to their inclination.—
Those strikers will be of great use at the pinch of the game, as
many of them will do to head companies; and there will be no danger in them, when they are to go immediately to work, and have the
prospect of wealth before them; there are many of them who will
fight like Turks.

Our black emissaries have the promise of a share in the spoils we
may gain, and we promise to conduct them to Texas should we be
defeated, where they will be free; but we never talk of being defeated. We always talk of victory and wealth to them. There is
no danger of any man, if you can ever get him once implicated, or
engaged in a matter. That is the way we employ our strikers in all
things: we have them implicated before we trust them from our
sight.

This may seem too bold to you, Hues; but that is what I glory
in. All the crimes I have ever committed, have been of the most
daring nature; and I have been successful in all my attempts, as yet;
and I am confident that I will be victorious in this matter, as to the
robberies which I have in contemplation; and I will have the pleasure and honor of seeing and knowing that my management has
glutted the earth with more human gore, and destroyed more property than any other robber who has ever lived in America, or the
known world. I look on the American people as my common enemy. They have disgraced me, and they can do no more: my life
is nothing to me, and it shall be spent as their devoted enemy. My
clan is strong, brave, and experienced; and is rapidly increasing in
strength every day. I should not be surprised, if it were to be two
thousand strong by the 25th of Decemder, 1835; and in addition to
this, I have the advantage of any other leader of a banditti that has
ever preceded me, for there is at least one half of my grand council who are men of high standing; and many of them in honorable
and lucrative offices. Should any thing leak out by chance, these

men would crush it at once, by ridiculing the idea and fears of the
people. They would soon make it a humbug, cock, tail, and a bull
story; and all things accounted for, to the satisfaction of the community, short order. Hues, how do you suppose that I understood
your disposition so quick, and drew you out on the subject of speculation, so that I could get your sentiments in so short a time after
we got in company?

Hues. That is what I do not understand, and I can only account
for it, as I would many other of your unrivalled performances, by
attributing it to your great knowledge and experience of the world,
and of mankind.

M. I had not been in company with you more than two hours,
before I knew you as well as if I had made you; and could have
trusted my life in your hands; for d——d if I could not see hell
dance in your eyes. A little practice is all you want, and you can
look into the very heart and thoughts of a man.

The art of learning men is nothing, when you once see how it is
managed. You must commence in this way: Begin to tell of some
act of villainy, and notice the answers and countenance of the man
as you go on with your story; and if you discover him to lean a
little, you advance a little; but if he recedes, you withdraw, and
commence some other subject; and if you have carried the matter
a little too far before you have learned him, by being too anxious,
make a jest of it, and pass it off in that way.

H. I cannot see how you will provide the negroes with arms to
fight with.

M. We have a considerable amount of money, in the hands of
our treasurers for the purpose of purchasing arms and ammunition,
to fit out the companies that are to attack the cities and banks, and
we will manage to get possession of the different arsenals, and supply ourselves from every source that may offer. We can get, from
every house we enter, more or less supplies of this kind, until we
will be well supplied. The negroes that scour the country settle-
ments will not want many arms until they can get them from the
houses they destroy, as an axe, a club, or knife, will do to murder a
family at a late hour in the night, when all are sleeping. There will
be but little defence made the first night by the country people, as
all will be confusion and alarm, for the first day or two, until the
whites can embody.

The weather was so very cold that Hues began to insist on stopping until day, as they had rode until a late hour in the night, and
Hues felt like freezing; but Murel never complained the first time
of being cold. They stopped at a good looking house, and so soon
as they were warm, they were lit to their lodgings—the place will
never be forgot by Hues. It was a large open room, and the bed-
tick was stuffed with corn shucks, which made as much noise when
they got in, as riding a new saddle. The covering consisted of a
thin coverlid, and cotton counterpane. Murel lay and cursed the

landlord all night, and Hues lay and shivered like he had a hard ague until morning. Next morning Murel enquired for the bill—there were twelve pence each, for lodging. "What!" says Murel, "a 'leven-penny-bit for riding such a colt as we rode last night—he has not been curried since the day he was foaled ; d——d high for lodging on the shuck pen. Here is the money, sir. Come, Hues, we will be travelling, I am not fond of roughness, although it is winter."

CHAPTER V.

Murel and Hues were on the road before sunrise the next morning, notwithstanding the disagreeable night they had spent at their late landlord's. Murel expressed a great anxiety to reach Arkansaw that night, before he slept. Murel having disclosed his plans to his young friend, and as he thought, completely captivated his feelings and fancy with the prospect of inexhaustible wealth, and viewing him as already entered into participation of his bloody designs, proposed to give him a short history of his life, commencing at ten years old.

Murel. I was born in middle Tennessee. My parents had not much property ; but they were intelligent people ; and my father was an honest man I expect, and tried to raise me honest ; but I think none the better of him for that. My mother was of the pure girt : she learnt me and all her children to steal so soon as we could walk, and would hide for us whenever she could. At ten years old I was not a bad hand. The first good haul I made was from a pedlar who lodged at my father's house one night. I had several trunk keys, and in the night I unlocked one of his trunks and took a bolt of linen and several other things, and then locked the trunk. The pedlar went off before he discovered the trick ; I thought that was not a bad figure I had made. About this time there was some pains taken with my education. At the age of sixteen I played a trick on a merchant in that country. I walked into his store one day, and he spoke to me very polite, and called me by the name of a young man who had a rich father, and invited me to trade with him. I thanked him, and requested him to put down a bolt of superfine cloth ; I took a suit and had it charged to the rich man's son.

I began to look after larger spoils, and run several fine horses.— By the time I was twenty, I began to acquire considerable character as a villain, and I concluded to go off and do my speculation where I was not known, and go on a larger scale ; so I began to see the value of having friends in this business. I made several associates ; I had been acquainted with some old hands for a long time, who had gave me the names of some royal fellows between Nashville and **Tuscaloosa**, and between Nashville and Savannah, in the State of Georgia, and many other places. Myself and a fellow by the name of Crenshaw gathered four good horses, and started for Georgia. We got in company with a young South Carolinian just before we got to Cumberland mountain, and Crenshaw soon knew all about his business. He had been to Tennessee to buy a drove of hogs, but when he got there pork was dearer than he had calculated, and he declined purchasing. We concluded he was a prize. Crenshaw winked at me, I understood his idea. Crenshaw had travelled the road before, but I never had ; we had travelled several miles on the mountain, when we passed near a great precipice ; just before we passed it Crenshaw asked me for my whip, which had a pound of lead in the butt, I handed it to him and he rode up by the side of the South Carolinian, and gave him a blow on the side of the head and tumbled him from his horse ; we lit from our horses and fingered his pockets ; we got twelve hundred and sixty-two dollars. Crenshaw said he knew of a place to hide him, and gathered him under the arms and me by his feet, and conveyed him to a deep crevice in the brow of the precipice, and tumbled him into it, he went out of sight ; we then tumbled in his saddle, and took his horse with us, which was worth two hundred dollars. We turned our course for South Alabama, and sold our horses for a good price. We frolicked for a week or more, and was the highest larks you ever saw. We commenced sporting and gambling, and lost every d——d cent of our money.

We was forced to resort to our profession for a second raise.— We stole a negro man and pushed for Mississippi. We had promised him that we would conduct him to a free State, if he would let us sell him one time, as we went on the way ; we agreed to give him part of the money. We sold him for six hundred dollars ; but when we went to start, the negro seemed to be very uneasy and appeared to doubt our coming back for him, as we had promised.— We lay in a creek bottom, not far from the place where we had sold the negro all the next day, and after dark we went to the china tree, in the lane, where we were to meet Tom ; he had been waiting for some time. He mounted his horse, and we pushed with him a second time. We rode twenty miles that night to the house of a friendly speculator. I had seen him in Tennessee, and had give him several lifts. He gave me his place of residence, so I might find him when I was passing. He is quite rich, and one of the best kind of fellows. Our horses were fed what they would eat, and two of them was foundered the next morning. We were detained a few days, and during that time our friend went to a little village in the neighborhood, and saw the negro advertised, and a description of the two men, of whom he had been purchased ; and giving his suspicions of the men. It was rather squally times, but any port in a storm ; we took the negro that night on the bank of a creek which runs by the farm of our friend, and Crenshaw shot him through the head. We took out his entrails, and sunk him in the creek; our friend furnished us with one fine horse, and we left him our foundered horses. We made our way through the Choctaw and Chickasaw nations, and then to Williamson county, in this State. We had made a d——d fine trip, if we had taken care of all we made.

I had become a considerable libertine, and when I returned home, I spent a few months rioting in all the luxuries of forbidden pleasure with the girls of my acquaintance.

My stock of cash was soon gone, and put to my shift for more. I commenced with horses, and run several from the adjoining counties; I had got associated with a young man who had got to be a circuit preacher among the Methodists, and a sharper he was; he was as slick on the tongue as goose grease. I took my first lessons in divinity from this young preacher. He was highly respected by all that knew him, and well calculated to please; he first put me in the notion of preaching to aid me in my speculation.

I got into difficulties about a mare that I had taken, and was imprisoned for near three years. I shifted it from court to court, but I was at last found guilty, and whipped. During my confinement I read the scriptures, and became a good judge of scripture. I had not neglected the criminal laws for many years before that time.— When they turned me loose I was prepared for any thing; I wanted to kill all but my own grit; and one of them I will die by his side before I will desert him.

My next speculation, was in the Choctaw nation. Myself and brother stole two fine horses, and made our way into the Choctaw nation. We got in with an old negro man and his wife and three sons to go with us to Texas, and promised them that if they would work for us one year after we got there, that we would let them go free, and told them many fine stories. We got into the Mississippi swamp, and was badly bothered to reach the bank of the river.— We had turned our horses loose at the edge of the swamp, and let them go to hell. After we reached the bank of the river we were in a bad condition, as we had no craft to convey us down the river, and our provisions gave out, and our only means for a support was killing varments and eating them. Eventually we found an Indian trail through the bottom, and we followed it to a bayou that made into the river, and we had the pleasure of finding a large canoe locked to the bank; we broke it loose and rowed into the main river, and were soon descending the river for New Orleans.

The old negro man became suspicious that we were going to sell them, and became quite contrary. We saw it would not do to have him with us; so we landed one day by the side of an island, and I requested him to go with me around the point of the island to hunt a good place to catch some fish; after we were obscured from our company I shot him through the head, and then ripped open his belly and tumbled him into the river! I returned to my company and told them that the old negro had fallen into the river, and that he never came up after he went under. We landed fifty miles above New Orleans, went into the country and sold our negroes to a Frenchman for nineteen hundred dollars.

We went from where we sold the negroes to New Orleans, and dressed ourselves like young lords. I mixed with the loose characters of the *swamp* every night. One night, as I was returning to the tavern where I boarded, I was stopped by two armed men, who demanded my money. I handed them my pocket book, and observed that I was very happy to meet with them, as we were all of the same profession. One of them observed, "d——d if I ever rob a brother-chip. We have had our eyes on you and the man that has generally come with you, for several nights: we saw so much rigging and glittering jewelry, that we concluded you must be some wealthy dandy, with surplus of cash, and had determined to rid you of the trouble of some of it; but if you are a robber, here is your pocket book, and you must go with us to-night, and we will give you an introduction to several fine fellows of the block—but stop, do you understand this motion!" I answered it, and thanked them for their kindness, and turned with them. We went to old mother Surgick's and had a real frolic with her girls. That night was the commencement of my greatness, in what the world calls villainy. The two fellows who robbed me, were named Haines and Phelps; they made me known to all the speculators that visited New Orleans; and gave me the name of every fellow who would speculate, that lived on the Mississippi river, and many of its tributary streams from New Orleans up to all the large western cities.

I had become acquainted with a Kentuckian, who boarded at the same tavern I did, and suspected he had a large sum of money; I felt an inclination to count it for him before I left the city; so I made my notions known to Phelps and my other new comrades, and concerted our plan. I was to get him off to the *swamp* with me on a spree, and when we were returning to our lodgings, my friends were to meet us and rob us both. I had got very intimate with the Kentuckian, and he thought me one of the best fellows in the world. He was very fond of wine; and I had him well fumed with good wine before I made the proposition for a frolic. When I invited him to walk with me, he readily accepted the invitation. We cut a few shines with the girls, and started to the tavern. We were met by a band of robbers, and robbed of all our money. The Kentuckian was so mad, that he cursed the whole city, and wished that it would all be deluged in a flood of water, so soon as he left the place. I went to my friends the next morning, and got my share of the spoil money, and my pocket book that I had been robbed of. We got seven hundred and five dollars from the bold Kentuckian, which was divided among thirteen of us.

I commenced travelling and making all the acquaintances among the speculators that I could. I went from New Orleans to Cincinnati, and from there I visited Lexington, in Kentucky. I found a

speculator about four miles from Newport, who furnished me with
a fine horse, the second night after I arrived at his house. I went
from Lexington to Richmond, in Virginia, and from there I visited
Charleston in the State of South Carolina; and from thence to
Milledgville, by the way of Savannah and Augusta, in the State of
Georgia. I made my way from Milledgville to Williamson county,
the old stamping ground. In all the route I only robbed eleven
men ; but I preached some d——d fine sermons, and scattered some
counterfeit United States' paper among my brethren.

The day passed off, and Murel was not through the history of his
life ; though he was hindered in the latter part of the day, by finding his road, or rather trail, in the Mississippi bottom, impassible from
high waters. He was compelled to go higher up the river for a
crossing place. He made several efforts to get on but could not
succeed. They concluded to stop at a house on the river, until they
had the light of another day. The landlord where they staid was
named John Champeon, a character who deserves the confidence of
his country for his conduct in this matter. Murel soon began to
feel of Mr. Champeon on the subject of speculation, as he chooses
to call it, by telling the wonderful deeds of those two young men of
Madison county. Here Hues had the pleasure of re-hearing nearly
the same stories which had constituted the introduction between
him and Murel ; but Mr. Champeon was not so well prepared to receive them as what Hues was. The conversation between Murel
and Mr. Champeon that night, enabled Hues to judge of the character of Mr. Champeon ; and he needed a man on that occasion,
in whose hands he could trust the care of his life ; and he found the
very character he wanted in Mr. Champeon. Murel and Mr.
Champeon continued their conversation until late bed time, on the
subject of speculation. Murel made a great many enquiries about
his clan that lived along on the river, and wanted to know of Mr.
Champeon how the Loyds, Barneys, and many others stood, as honorable men: representing himself as an entire stranger to them, and
the country they lived in ; and said that his business over among
them was to collect some money which was owing to him.

After Murel and Hues were retired to their bed chamber, Murel
wanted to know of Hues, how he liked the way he had managed
their landlord? to which Hues replied, that none could have managed him better. Murel then informed Hues that they would be
compelled to leave their horses with Mr. Champeon, and work
their way through the swamp on foot, until they could get a skiff to
convey them to his friends, on the other side of the river; and said
that they would be dependent on Mr. Champeon, and that he could
see Mr. Champeon was hell on the speculators ; and for that reason
he had pretended to know nothing about the people on the other
side of the river, as an acquaintance with them would be good
grounds for him to suspect them for going after no good. Murel
changed his name to Merel, and gave his residence in Williamson

county, instead of Madison county, and assumed the character of a negro trader, while conversing with Mr. Champeon.

The next morning after breakfast at Mr. Champeon's, Murel and Hues started down the bank of the river on foot, to find some person who had a skiff to hire. After they had gone three hundred yards or more, Hues told Murel that he had left his gloves at the house, and that it was so cold that he would be compelled to have them—so he requested Murel to wait for him until he went after them. Murel seated himself on a log, and Hues went back to the house. Hues had left his gloves on purpose that he might have an excuse to return to the house without the company of Murel.— Hues wished to have a private conversation with Mr. Champeon, and he knew it would not do to let Murel see him conversing privately with any person, as it might excite his suspicion, and get himself into the worst of difficulties, after he would be surrounded by Murel's friends, in the wild morass where they were trying to go.— Hues apprized Mr. Champeon of his business, and of his adventure, in as few words as possible ; and gave him his ideas concerning getting a knowledge where the Parson's negroes were, and then getting a guard and going and taking them and the thieves, if he could get off from Murel, after being conveyed to the negroes ; or so near them, that he could find the place after he had got a guard to assist him. Hues wished to learn the place where the negroes were, without seeing them, or rather being seen by them, as they would know him, and make his true name known to Murel and his friends ; and he considered such a developement would be very dangerous in so unfriendly a place. Mr. Champeon assured Hues that he should have all the assistance which it was in his power to give ; and told him that he would collect fifty men, if he could make any discoveries where the negroes were. Mr. Champeon cautioned Hues of the great danger which he was then going to encounter in his adventure ; and gave him an elegant pocket pistol. Hues then had three good pistols to defend himself: provided he should be carried to the Parson's negroes, and discovered before he could get off. His plan was to take the advantage, and get the first shot, should he be discovered as a spy ; and in that way make his three pistols supply the place of men, should he have an equal number to contend with ; which he was compelled to look for. When Hues was disclosing his adventure to Mr. Champeon, he evidently showed that he was alarmed ; and he has since declared, that he felt more of the effects of fear, in that matter, than he ever had in all his life before. It was the idea of placing his life in the hands of a man whom he had never seen until the night before, that caused his fears ; for he well knew, that if the man was not an honest man, or had the least friendship for villainy, he would apprize the friends of Murel of the character he had in company, and give them a chance to devise any means for the destruction of both his life and character, as none of his friends knew the course he was pursuing with Murel ;

but Hues was not mistaken in the notions he had formed of Mr. Champeon. Hues gave Mr. Champeon his real name, and requested him not to let Murel's horse go if he sent for him, until he first knew that there was no accident happened to him, from Murel and his clan ; and Hues further instructed Mr. Champeon, if Murel returned for his horse, and he was not with him, to take Murel immediately, as that would be evidence sufficient, that he was murdered or detained by the clan. Mr. Champeon promised to attend to all of his requests. Hues was not willing for Murel to escape justice any longer. He had heard him recount the black deeds of his life, until his blood had frequently chilled, and his heart sickened to hear his horrid deeds and purposes related. He was devotedly disposed to hazard his own life to the greatest dangers to accomplish the capture of so obdurate a villain, whose only study, and purpose of life, was the destruction of the human family, and their property.

Hues returned to Murel, where he was seated on the log at the bank of the river, and they proceeed on their journey ; after considerable toil and difficulty, they succeeded in crossing the slues, and reached the house of a Mr. Irvin, three miles below Mr. Champeon's, but the skiff that Mr. Irvin had been using was sent home, three miles below Mr. Irvin's and there was a lake between them ; so they were compelled to stop for the want of a craft. They concluded to wait a day or two, and see if a trading boat would pass, that would convey them down the river to where the skiff was.— Murel and Hues were prevented from conversing very much at Mr. Irvin's, as he had no private room. They remained at Mr. Irvin's until the next evening, when a small trading boat landed, on which they got a passage down the river to where the skiff was. During the time they were at Mr. Irvin's, Murel was feeling Mr. Irvin on the subject of speculation, in the same way he did Mr. Champeon, and represented himself as a negro trader. He was so smooth on the tongue that Mr. Irvin believed every word he said ; and even proposed to purchase three negro men from Mr. Merel as he called himself.

Mr. Merel was to deliver Mr. Irvin three likely negro men, in three weeks, at six hundred dollars each. Mr. Champeon had recommended Mr. Irvin to Hues, as a man whom he might depend on in any matter whatever ; and after all their bargain was made, as far as it could be made until the delivery of the negroes, Hues made a chance to have a private conversation with Mr. Irvin, and acquainted him with his adventure ; and solicited his assistance, provided he should need it, which was readily promised by Mr. Irvin.

Hues had a blank book in his pocket, which he would tear into small pieces, on which he kept a journal of Murel's confessions, plans, designs and life, as he related it himself. He tore the paper into small pieces not larger than a dollar. This he done to avoid suspicion on the part of Murel ; as if he had seen Hues writing in a book he would have suspected him for making a record, which would have been very apt to have produced bad consequences on the part of Hues and his adventure. Hues would frequently write proper names and places on his boot legs, finger nails, saddle skirts, and portmanteau, with a needle, as he would be riding and listening to Murel's horrid account of himself. This he done to aid his memory when he come to commit it to paper. When he would fill both sides of one of his scraps of paper, he numbered and stowed it away in the crown of his cap. He wrote his journal in stenography. While Murel and Hues was at the house of Mr. Irvin, Hues had an opportunity of walking out and arranging memorandums in such order as could be understood. In this cautious manner Hues succeeded in retaining a correct journal of all that occurred, while on the disagreeable and dangerous travels with John A. Murel, the great Western Land Pirate.

Murel and Hues landed at the house of a Mr. Hargues : where they got the promise of a skiff the next morning ; but the next morning brought with it a snow storm, which detained them all the day, and until the next morning ; making in all better than three days they were detained in travelling six miles. Murel became very impatient, and would swear that the devil had quit cutting his cards for him ; that the d——d old preacher's negroes had cost him more trouble and perplexity of mind, than any he had ever stolen in all his life. When Murel and Hues would be walking on the bank of the river, Murel would frequently wonder where young Henning was, and say that he would give five hundred dollars to find him over in Arkansaw hunting him ; and would tell how he would have him tortured by his clan. He told Hues that Henning had been so officious, and had let his tongue run so much about him and his brother, that he was not satisfied with stealing his negroes alone, but that he had got one of his clan to head a company of friends that intended to go to young Henning's house some night, and take him out of his bed and give him two hundred and fifty lashes ; and as he knew that they would suspect him for it, he intended to stay at a tavern in Jackson on the night it would take place. He said that the man on whom he had pitched for a leader of the company was named Eli Chandler, a second Cæsar. Hues would scarcely be able to contain himself when he would hear Murel telling how he would beat his young friend.

Murel and Hues were ready for a start from Mr. Hargues' the second morning after breakfast, having been detained one day and night longer in consequence of the snow storm. They landed on the Arkansaw side, and then Murel led the way through the swamp for the council house. They had travelled three hours in the bottom, part of the way on foot, and part in skiffs, and had passed several small huts in the canebrakes on the way, which were occupied by men and sometimes by negroes : When Murel pointed to a large cotton tree which stood in towering height, and stupendous size, over all the other timber around it, and said to Hues, "do you see you lofty cotton wood that rises so majestically over all the other timber?" Hues replied that he did. "Well," said Murel, "that tree stands in the garden of Eden, and we only have a quarter of a mile to go, and then we will be on the happy spot, where many a noble plot has been concerted." Hues had been expecting to come to the hut where the Parson's negroes were secreted in this wild morass, and had muffled his face in his handkerchief as if his face was cold, but it was to prevent the negroes from knowing him, provided he should come on them. They arrived at the council house and found eleven of the clan who had come in for a supply of counterfeit money, and to learn how each other were managing the concerns of the clan, and whether any brothers were imprisoned, and needed the assistance of the clan to relieve them; and how many proselytes each member had made ready for admittance.— Hues felt a considerable damp come over him as he entered the horrid hovel at the back of Murel. The clan was very anxious to know the reason why Murel had not attended at the council house at the time he had promised his striker to meet him. To which Murel replied that he was too strongly suspected for the very thing that he had done to start at the appointed time, and then that he was detained by high water. They informed him that his negroes had arrived, and that they were badly frost bit, and that they had become uneasy about him and thought it best to push them and make sales as soon as possible. Compliments and questions being over between Murel and his clan, Murel called the attention of the house, and then took Hues by the hand, and presented him to the company with the following remarks: "Here my brave counsellors, this is a counsellor of my own making, and I am not ashamed of the workmanship. Let Mr. Hues be examined by whom he may." They all shook hands with Hues, and then gave him the two degrees in signs, which belongs to the two classes. He first received the sign of the striker, and then of the grand counsellor. The signs are a particular pressure and flirt of the hand. Hues was practiced by them until he could give and receive the signs as well as any of them.

Hues was then requested to give them his opinion concerning the negro war, and what he conceived to be their faith. The following is an extract from the address which was delivered them by Hues, while in their council house.

"*An extract from Adam Hues' Speech in Mystic Council.*

Gentlemen of the Mystic conspiracy—my age and inexperience must plead my excuse before this worthy and experienced congregation. I am much better qualified to acquiesce in the measures and sentiments of others, than to advance principles of my own on this important occasion. It has been so recent that I was honored with the secrets of this august conspiracy, that I can advance nothing original, as all my ideas have been received from our honorable

39

dictator, and I should deem it presumption in me to offer any
amendments to the present deep and well arranged plans and purposes of his majesty. My opinion is, that your plans are entirely
practicable, under the guidance of our experienced leader.

As to what I consider to be the faith and principle of this noble
and lordly band is easily related, and I expect it is correct: as my
sentiments are modeled by his majesty, and I consider myself nothing more than a creature of his formation in this noble conspiracy.
I consider that the members of this conspiracy are absolved from
every other power or obligation to either God or man: we found
ourselves placed in the world, surrounded with every thing needful
for our comfort and enjoyment: and shall we stand supinely by and
see others enjoy, and make no provisions for ourselves, because an
established religious and moral custom, which we neither believe or
respect, forbids us from choosing the mode of providing. We consider all that are under the control of our power as our right; and
more, we consider man, earth and beast, all as materials subject to
the enterprise of our power. Turn your attention to the animal
world; do we not see the beasts of the field, the fowls of the air,
and the fish in the sea, all in their turns falling a victim to each other: and last of all, turn your attention to man, and do we not see
him falling a victim to his fellow-man? Yes, sirs, if there is any
God, these are his laws; but my noble sirs, we acknowledge no moral restrictions apart from the fraternity. Yes, my worthy sirs, we
will live the lords of our own wills, rioting in all the pompous luxuries which the spoils of our enemies and opposers will afford.

We are told by history, that Rome lost her liberty by the conspiracy of three Romans on an island of the river Panalious; and why
not the conspiracy of four hundred Americans in this morass of the
Mississippi river, glean the Southern and Western Banks, destroy
their cities, and slaughter our enemies? Have we no Cassius to
scatter the fire-brands of rebellion; no Lepidus to open his coffers
of gold: and no Augustus to lead us to battle? Such a conclusion
would go to impeach the abilities of our gallant chieftain."

Murel having some business to arrange with some of his clan who
were not at the council house, left the company, and he and Hues
went to the house of G. Barney that evening. Murel made an arrangement with his friends concerning the negroes he was to bring
to Mr. Irvin. Murel was to bring the negroes and get his eighteen
hundred dollars, and the next night his friends were to go over the
river in a skiff to a certain point, where the negroes were to be placed ready for the skiff to carry them from the unfortunate purcha-
ser to some other market to repeat the fraud. Hues having discovered that the Parson's negroes were sent off, and that there were
no further discoveries to be made by his remaining among the robbers without enquiring to what market they were sent, and that he
deemed imprudent in that horrid place, as a very small matter
might lead to suspicion, and examination, which would have been

certain destruction, as Hues had many papers with him which would have condemned him before a court of pirates and murderers ; so Hues began to plan to get an excuse to return to Mr. Irvin's and wait for Murel until he was through with the business of the fraternity. Hues made choice of his excuse to urge before Murel, and proposed his wishes to him, but Murel was opposed to his going until he went himself, and urged many reasons in opposition to his wishes. The excuse that Hues made for wishing to return to Mr. Irvin's, was to get acquainted with a lady who lived at Mr. Irvin's house, which he urged as the best of reasons, and the more he thought on the matter, the more he was determined to go, for he could see no cause why he should continue to hazard his life to so many dangers when neither his old friend nor his country were to be benefited by so doing. Murel urged that he wanted to see him have some sport with the Arkansaw girls before he returned ; and that there were several matters before the council, which he wished to hear his opinion on. To these wishes of Murel's Hues replied, that as to the girls he could dispense with them for the present, under existing circumstances ; and as to his opinion in council he hoped to be excused for the present, as he was not prepared to give any ideas of his own, and assured Murel that he had the utmost confidence in his opinion on any matter which might be agitated before the house, and preferred it to his own. Murel's vanity being flattered by the encomiums passed on his opinions, consented to the arrangements made by Hues, and saw him safe across the river before they parted.

Hues returned to Mr. Irvin's, and Murel to the business of his profession. Hues felt quite relieved to find himself once more among honest people, after passing through the hands of so many cut-throats, in a morass, which has associated with it all that the fancy can select from the whole school of horrors; and I would say, from the description given by Hues, an emblem of that awful place, allotted to rebellious and wicked spirits, in the world of misery, and its fiendish courts.

Hues concerted a plan with Mr. Irvin, to have a guard at his house at the time Murel was to bring him the negroes, to secure Murel and the negroes he might bring with him ; and in that way capture the mighty man of the West, as he did not know that his confessions would be sufficient evidence against him, and Hues was well aware that if the evidence depended entirely on himself, that it would be the greatest inducement for so extensive a banditti to unite and exert all their power for his destruction, as they would know that the fate of their favorite designs and daring leader would depend on their success in that matter : for this reason alone, Hues was anxious that he should be taken in the act of delivering the negroes, which he had promised to deliver to Mr. Irvin in three weeks: but the marvellous manner in which Hues become master of Murel's secrets and plans, were another inducement with him, that other evidence should be had before Murel was arrested, as that would remove the burthen of evidence from himself.

The next evening, after Hues had returned to Mr. Irvin's, Murel came; and after he and Mr. Irvin had talked over their trade about the negroes, and fixed on the time when they were to be delivered, Murel and Hues returned to Mr. Champeon's that evening, where they had left their horses, after being gone six days. Hues had no opportunity to have any private conversation with Mr. Champeon concerning his adventure, but got an opportunity to hand him the pistol which had been given to him by Mr. Champeon, before he entered the morass. Murel and Hues left Mr. Champeon's the next morning after breakfast and directed their course for Madison county.

Murel began to talk of the bad luck which he was having with the old Parson's negroes, and Hues for the first time ventured to ask him a direct question, after trying many indirect questions, and failing to get the information which he wanted. He then asked Murel to what market his friends had sent the negroes, which he had taken from the Methodist preacher. To which Murel replied: "They have sent my two, and three other fellows, and seven horses, down the river, in one of those small trading boats, and they intended to go through the Choctaw pass if they could, to the Yazoo market; and they have ten thousand dollars in counterfeit money, which I expect is to upset the whole matter. I am not pleased with the arrangement. The fellows whom they have sent are only strikers, and that is too much to put into their hands at one time. D——d if I am not fearful they will think themselves made men when they sell, and leave us behind in the lurch; though Loyd says there is no danger in them: and he told them to sell and misle."*

Murel and Hues being once more to themselves on the road, Murel re-commenced the history of his life as follows:

Murel. "After I returned home from the first grand circuit I made among the speculators, I remained at home a very short time, as I could not rest when my mind was not actively engaged in some speculation. I had commenced the foundation of this mystic clan on that tour, and suggested the plan of exciting a rebellion among the negroes as the sure road to an inexhaustible fortune to all who would engage in the expedition. The first mystic sign which is used by this clan, was in use among robbers before I was born; and the second had its origin from myself, Phelps, Haines, Cooper, Doris, Bolton, Harris, Doddridge, Celly, Morris, Walter, Depont, and one of my brothers, on the second night after my acquaintance with them in New Orleans. We needed a higher order to carry on our designs, and we adopted the sign, and called it the sign of the grand council of the mystic clan; and practised ourselves to give and receive the new sign to a fraction, before we parted: and in addition

* The word misle, as used above, the reader must judge of the intended meaning: as Hues was not inquisitive enough to enquire of Murel, what he meant by that expression.

to this improvement, we invented and formed a mode of corresponding by means of ten characters, mixed with other matter, which has been very convenient on many occasions, and especially when any of us gets into difficulties. I was encouraged in my new undertaking, and my heart began to beat high with the hope of being able, one day, to visit the pomp of the southern and western people, in my vengeance ; and of seeing their cities and towns one common scene of devastation, smoked walls and fragments.

I decoyed a negro man from his master in Middle Tennessee, and sent him to Mills' Point by a young man, and I waited to see the movements of the owner.

He thought his negro had run off. So I started to take possession of my prize. I got another friend at Mills' Point to take my negro in a skiff and convey him to the mouth of Red River, and I took a passage on a steamboat. I then went through the country by land, and sold my negro for nine hundred dollars, and the second night after I stole him again, and my friend run him to the Irish bayou in Texas ; I followed on after him, and I sold my negro in Texs for five hundred dollars. I then concluded to visit South America, and see if there was no opening in that country for a speculation ; and I had concluded that I could get some strong friends in that country to aid me in my designs relative to a negro rebellion ; but of all the people in the world, the Spaniards are the most treacherous and cowardly ; I never want them concerned in any matter with me, I had rather take the negroes in this country to fight, than a Spaniard. I stopped in a village and passed as a doctor, and commenced practising medicine. I could ape the doctor first rate, having read Ewel, and several other works on primitive medicine. I became a great favorite of an old Catholic ; he adopted me as his son in the faith, and introduced me to all the best families as a young doctor from North America. I had been with the old Catholic but a very short time, before I was a great Roman Catholic ; and bowed to the cross, and attended regular to all the ceremonies of that persuasion, and to tell you the fact, Hues, all that the Catholic requires or needs, to be universally received, is to be correctly represented ; but you know that I care nothing about religion ; I had been with the old Catholic about three months, and was getting a heavy practice, when an opportunity offered for me to rob the old Catholic's secretary of nine hundred dollars in gold, and could have got as much more in silver, if I could have carried it. I was soon on the road for home again ; I stopped three weeks in New Orleans as I came on home, and had some high fun with old mother Surgick's girls.

I collected all my friends about New Orleans, at one of our friends houses in that place, and we set in coucil three days, before we got all our plans to our notion ; we then determined to undertake the rebellion at every hazard, and make as many friends as we could for that purpose. Every man's business being assigned him, I started to Natchez on foot ; having sold my horse in New Orleans, with the intention of stealing another after I started; I walked four days, and no opportunity offered for me to get a horse. The fifth day, about twelve o'clock I had become very tired, and stopped at a creek to get some water, and rest a little. While I was sitting on a log, looking down the road the way I had come, a man come in sight riding a good looking horse. The very moment I saw him I was determined to have his horse, if he was in the garb of a traveller.— He rode up, and I saw from his equippage, that he was a traveller. I arose from my seat, and drew an elegant rifle pistol on him, and ordered him to dismount. He done so, and I took his horse by the bridle, and pointed down the creek, and ordered him to walk before me. We went a few hundred yards and stopped. I hitched his horse, then made him undress himself all to his shirt and drawers, and ordered him to turn his back to me; he asked me if I was going to shoot him. I ordered him the second time to turn his back to me. He said, "if you are determined to kill me, let me have time to pray before I die." I told him I had no time to hear him pray. He turned round and dropped on his knees, and I shot him through the back of the head. I ripped open his belly and took out his entrails, and sunk him in the creek. I then searched his pockets, and found four hundred and one dollars and thirty-seven cents, and a number of papers that I did not take time to examine. I sunk the pocket book and papers, and hat in the creek. His boots were brand new, and fit me very genteel, and I put them on, and sunk my old shoes in the creek to atone for them. I rolled up his clothes and put them into his portmanteau, as they were brand new cloth, of the best quality. I mounted as fine a horse as ever I straddled, and directed my course for Natchez in much better style than I had been for the last five days.

I reached Natchez, and spent two days with my friends at that place, and the girls under the hill together. I then left Natchez for the Choctaw Nation, with the intention of giving some of them a chance for their property. As I was riding along, between Benton and Rankin, planning for my designs, I was overtaken by a tall and good looking young man, riding an elegant horse: which was splendidly rigged off; and the young gentleman's apparel was of the richest that could be had, and his watch chain and other jewelry were of the richest and best. I was anxious to know if he intended to travel through the Choctaw Nation, and soon managed to learn. He said he had been to the lower country with a drove of negroes, and was returning home to Kentucky. We rode on, and soon got very intimate for strangers, and agreed to be company through the Indian Nation. We were two d——d fine looking men, and to hear us talk we were very rich. I felt of him on the subject of speculation, but d——n it, how he cursed the speculators, and said that he was in a bad condition to fall into the hands of such d——d villains, as he had the cash with him that twenty negroes had sold for; and that he was very happy that he had happened to get in company with me through the nation. I concluded that he was a noble prize, and longed to be counting his cash. At length we came into one of those long stretches in the nation, where there was no house for twenty miles, on the third day after we had been in company with each other. The country was high, hilly, and broken, and no water; just about the time I reached the place where I intended to count my companion's cash, I became very thirsty, and insisted on turning down a deep hollow, or dale, that headed near the road, to hunt some water. We had followed down the dale for near four hundred yards, when I drew my pistol and shot him through. He fell dead. I commenced hunting for his cash, and opened his large pocket book that was stuffed very full, and when I began to open it, I thought it a treasure indeed; but, Oh! the contents of that book; it was filled with the copies of songs, the forms of love letters, and some of his own composition—but no cash. I began to cut off his clothing with my knife, and examine them for his money. I found four dollars and a half in change, in his pockets, and no more. And is this the amount for which twenty negroes sold, thought I. I recollected his watch and jewelry, and I gathered them: his chain was rich and good, but it was swung to an old brass watch. He was a puff for true; and I thought all such d——d fools ought to die as soon as possible. I took his horse, and swapped him to an Indian native for four ponies, and sold them on the way home. I reached home, and spent a few weeks among the girls of my acquaintance, in all the enjoyments that money could afford.

My next trip was through Georgia, South Carolina, North Carolina, Virginia and Maryland, and then back to South Carolina, and from there round by Florida and Alabama. I began to conduct the progress of my operations, and establish my emissaries over the country in every direction. After I turned for home from Alabama, I was passing by where one of my friends lived, in company with three of my associates, who were going home with me; we stopped to see how our friend was doing; while we were sitting out in his portico, there was a large drove of sheep came up to his blocks. He went out and examined them, and found them to be the flock of an old Baptist, who lived about six miles up the road from his house, and they had been gone from their owner for three months, and he could hear nothing of them. The old Baptist had accused my friend of having his sheep drove off to market, and abused him for stealing his sheep very much. My friend acquainted me with the circumstance, and I concluded to play a trick on the old jockey for his suspicions, so we gathered up all the flock, and drove them on before us, and got to the old Baptist's just after dark; we called the old man out to the gate, and wanted to lodge with him all night; but he refused to take us in, and urged as a reason, that his old woman was sick, and he could not accommodate us as he would wish. To these objections I told him that we could wait on ourselves—that I had three active young men with me, who could do all that was wanting to be done. I told him that I had moved down below in the spring of the year, when my sheep was scattered, and I concluded to leave them until fall; and that I had been up to my old place after them, and was going home: and complained of the hard drive I had made that day, as an excuse to stop with the old Baptist. I then told him I had a very fine wether that I wished to kill, as he was very unruly, and hard to drive, and what we did not use that night he was welcome to. The old man shewed us a lot to pen our sheep, and the corn crib and stables, and told us that if we could wait on ourselves that we were welcome to stay. We soon fed our horses, and had the mutton dressed, and a large pot full cooking.— The old man told us where to find meal, milk and butter; and while my associates were cooking the sheep, I was conversing with the old Baptist on religion; I told him I was a Baptist preacher. When news came that the sheep was done, I went into the kitchen, and we had a real feast of mutton, at the expense of the old Baptist.

After supper we went in where the old lady was lying sick. The old man got his bible and hymn book, and invited me to go to duty. I used the books, and then prayed like hell for the recovery of the old lady. The next morning we were up before day-light, and had the sheep all on the road. We drove them about one mile, and scattered them in the woods, and left them.

We left the head of the wether that we killed lying in the lot where the old man could see that it was his own mark. I arrived at home after a trip of six months.

I have been going ever since from one place to another, directing and managing, but I have others now as good as myself to manage. This fellow, Phelps, that I was telling you of before, he is a noble fellow among the negroes, and he wants them all free; and he knows how to excite them as well as any person: but he will not do for a robber, as he cannot kill a man unless he has received an injury from him first; he is now in jail at Vicksburgh, and I fear will hang. I went to see him not long since: but he is so strictly watched, that nothing can be done. He has been in the habit of stopping men on the high-way and robbing them, and letting them go on; but that will never do for a robber: after I rob a man he will never give evidence against me; and there is but one safe plan in the business, and that is to kill—If I could not afford to kill a man I would not rob. I have often told Phelps he would be caught before he knew it. I could raise men enough to go and tear down the jail, and take Phelps by force; but that would endanger all of our other plans. I have frequently had money enough to have settled myself rich; but I have spent it as free as water in carrying on my designs. The last five years of my life have been spent in the same way that I have been telling you. Hues: I have been from home the best part of the time; and I have let but few chances escape me, when I could rob, that I did not do it. It would take a week, Hues, to tell over all of my scrapes of that kind. You must

come and stay at my house the week before I start with them negroes to Irvin, and I will have time to tell over all my ups and
downs for the last five years. I want you to go that trip with me.
You can arrange your business in the nation in two weeks, and get
to my house in Madison Conty. You will make more that trip
than all your concerns are worth in the nation, so you had better
give away what you have than to be confined to it."

Night having come on, Murel and Hues began to look out for a
house of entertainment; so Murel left off telling the horrid deeds of
his past life. They came to a house awhile after night, where they
stopped until morning.

The next morning Murel and Hues proceeded on their journey;
but the time was now drawing near when Murel was to loose his
young associate, as they had only ten miles to ride together, when
they would reach Wesley, there they were to part. Hues was to
go on to the nation, as Murel thought, to arrange his affairs to join
him again; and Murel was to go on home to procure the negroes
which he had promised to deliver to Mr. Irvin, and have them ready
by the time Hues was to be at his house, in Madison County. The
following is the last conversation of those two mystic friends, which
was enjoyed on the last ten miles.

M. "Well, Hues, we must part to-day; and I am not half done
talking, but I will quit telling what I have done, and tell what I am
going to do. I have about forty negroes now engaged, that are
waiting for me to run them, and the best of it is, they are the property of my enemies nearly entirely. I have a great many friends
who have got in to be overseers: they are a strong support to my
plan. I have a friend by the name of Nolin, my brother-in-law's
brother, who is overseeing in Alabama, for a man who is from home.
Nolin has decoyed six likely negro men for me, I am to go within
about ten miles with a two horse carryall, and stop at an appointed
place. Nolin is to raise a sham charge against the negroes, and
they are to run off and come to my waggon. I will put them into
the waggon: and fasten down the curtains all round, and then throw
fodder over them; and have a striker to drive them to the Mississippi swamp for me, where there will be no danger. I will ride a
few miles behind; but never seem to notice the waggon. Nolin is
to be driving the woods for the negroes, and reporting that he had
seen them every day or two, until I have time to get clear out of
the country with them. I have eight more engaged in Alabama, at
one Eason's, the fellow whom I was speaking of before. The remainder of the forty I get in my own country. You recollect the
boat that I showed you in the bayou, on the other side of the river?
that boat I intend to fill with negroes for my own benefit.

H. There is a fellow by the name of Bundles, or Burns, or some
such a name, a negro trader, who lives in some part of the new part
of Tennessee, who, I think, is as hard to cheat, as any man I have

ever seen in all my travels; and if all the Tennesseeans are as sharp as I think he is, I do not want to deal with many of them.

M. O! I know who you are thinking of, his name is Byrn; he does pass down through your country sometimes, and a hell of a fellow he is; he can cheat you to death, and make you think all the time he is putting you on the road to a fortune; but d——n him, I handled the cash that one of his negroes sold for. He suspected me for running his negro, and offered me the chance of him, for three hundred dollars; but I thought it was a d——d poor business to give three hundred dollars for a thing I already had. Byrn is a hard hand, and I had as soon fall into the hands of the Devil as his.

Hues spoke in this uncertain manner of the name of Mr. Byrn, to leave the impression on the mind of Murel, that he had just barely seen Mr. Byrn, and had only a faint conception of his name, without any acquaintance; yet so descriptive, as to make him understand whom he meant by his remarks. Hues knew that Byrn had lost a negro, and he wished to know whether Murel had stolen him or not; and he took the above ingenious plan to get Murel on the subject, without exciting his suspicion.

M. I can tell you another trick we have, Hues, to get horses.— Our friends examine the stray books regular, and whenever there is a stray horse of any value found on them, he goes and gets a description of the horse and then writes for two of his friends, if none do pass, who are strangers in the country he lives in. He gives his friends a minute description of the horse; and one will go and claim, and the other prove the property. I was in Arkansaw this fall, and there was a man who found a fine horse standing in the edge of the *M*ississippi river, which had by some means got off of some boat and swam to shore; but could not get up the bank; he dug the bank, and got out the horse. One of my friends heard of it, and went and examined the horse so that he could tell me all the flesh marks. I went and asked him if he had found a horse of such a description, describing the horse in every particular. He said he had. I looked at the horse and claimed him. I gave the fellow five dollars for his trouble, and took the horse home, and have him yet. I have swam the *M*ississippi twice on that horse.

H. We are not far from Wesley, where we will part, and you have not given me a list of the names of your friends as yet.

M. Oh! yes, yes. Have you any paper with you? you must have that before we part."

Hues took out the remainder of his blank book and pencil, which had not been used for a private record: When the following names were given, and recorded, as the friends and members of *M*urel's clan.

48

CATALOGUE OF MUREL'S MYSTIC CLAN.

Tennessee.

2—Murels,	S. Spires,	S. Weathers,
2—Byrdsongs,	D. Crenshaw,	Col. Jarot,
M. Dickson,	2—Nolins,	V. Chism,
Capt. Ruffin,	K. Dickson,	Ja. Hosskins,
L. Anderson,	W. Crenshaw,	P. Johnson,
J. Goaldin,	J. Nuckles,	R. Tims,
L. Bateman,	D. Ahart,	J. Taylor,
2—Busheys,	E. Chandler.	L. More
4—Maroneys',	J. Eas,	2—Littlepages,
W. Howel,	J. Hardin,	B. Sims,
Esq. Wilbern,	Z. Gorin,	Y. Pearson,
3—Boaltons',	G. Wiers,	G. Sparks,
5—Lathom's,	S. Larit,	A. Smith,
R. Parew,	6—Hueses',	K. Deron.

Mississippi.

G. Parker,	—Bloodworth,	S. Williams,
J. Durham,	R. Horton,	R. Forrow,
C. Hapes,	C. Cook,	W. Presley,
G. Goodman,	G. Corkle,	—Staunton,
B. Johnson,	—Clanin,	D. Rooker,
C. Hickman,	L. Cooper,	W. Thomas,
C. Barton,	Wm. Nawls,	5—Willeys',
D. Marlow,	J. Hess,	Capt. Medford,
2—Wilson's,	3—Hunters',	Capt. Morris,
2—Gilberts',	G. Tucker,	A. Brown,
3—Glenns',	4—Yarber's,	2—Harlins'.

Arkansaw.

S. Pucket,	2—Barneys',	W. Ray,
G. Aker,	J. Simmons,	4—Tuckers',
L. Good,	2—Lovds',	B. Norton,
3—Shurlocks',	J. Smith,	3—Joneses',
P. Billing,	L. Martin,	A. Hooper,
S. Coulter,	C. Jimerson,	H. Petit,
6—Serrils',	W. Henderson,	3—Bunches',
2—Nowlins',	4—Dartess',	3—Hortons'.

Kentucky.

3—Farrows',	D. Mugit,	2—Pattersons'.

4—Wards,   1—Foresythes,   S. Goin
  D. Clayton,   Q. Brantley,   R. Williamson,
  L. Potts,   H. Haly,   —Reeses',
  H. Potter,   3—Carters.

Missouri.

3—Whites,   W. Aker,   2—Herins,
2—Garlins,   6—Millers,   S. Falcon,
  G. Poap,   H. Warrin,   R. Coward,
3—Moaseways,   D. Corkle,   3—Johnsons,
  E. Boalin,   Col. S. W. Foreman.

Alabama.

H. Write,   W. Hickel,   J. Homes,
P. Miles,   G. Sheridon,   B. Corhoon,
O. Moore,   E. Nolin,   3—Parmers,
S. Baley,   2—Glascocks,   4—Sorils,
G. Hammons,   3—Martins,   R. Cunagen,
M. Hancock,   H. Chance,   Capt. Boin,
D. Belfer,   Esq. Malone.

Georgia.

H. Moris,   2—Heffils',   D. Haris,
D. Coalmon.   2—Rameys',   4—Reves',
4—Cullins',   6—Rosses',   W. Johnson,
  Capt. Ashley,   S. Gambel,   Denson, Esq.
2—Crenshaws',   2—Lenits',   4—Peakes'.

South Carolina.

3—Foarts',   W. Simpson,   2—Williams',
  E. Owin,   O. Russet,   2—Hookers',
  S. Pinkney,   3—Piles'   6—Woods',
  W. King,   H. Black,   N. Parsons,
  G. Hollier,   F. Waters,   3—Franklins,
  M. Ware,   G. Gravit,   4—Robertsons',
  B. Henry.

North Carolina.

A. Fentres,   J. Secel,   2—Micklejohns',
3—Hacks',   D. Harlison,   D. Barnet,
  M. Coopwood,   S. Bulkes,   R. Huiston,
  M. Johnson.   4—Solomons',   B. Kelit,

J. Hackey,	V. Miles,	S. Stogdon,
J. Haris,	3—Perrys',	L. Smith,
4—Gilferds',	K. Farmer,	W. Pariners.

Virginia.

R. Garrison,	J. Ferines,	A. Beloach,
G. Derom,	Kerkmon,	S. Walker,
3—Merits',	4—Mathises',	W. Carnes,
L. Wiseman,	D. Hawks,	S. Washorn,
P. Hume,	E. Cockburn,	F. Henderson,
W. Wilbern.		

Maryland.

W. Gwins,	2—Fishers',	H. Brown,
M. Hains,	F. Smith,	C. Paron,
G. Dortherd,	G. M'Waters,	L. Strawn,
A. Cuthbut,	3—Morgans',	W. Leemon,
D. Hays,	S. Winston,	4—Hobses,
D. Read,	H. M'Gleton,	M. O'Conel,
S. M'Write,	T. Goodin,	J. Wilkit.

Florida..

E. Carmefer,	C. Winkle,	W. Hargeret,
2—M'Gilits,	S. Whipel,	E. Foskew,
A. Sterling,	J. Deark,	B. Stafford,
J. Preston,	L. M'Guint,	3—Baggets'
G. Flush.		

Louisiana.

C. Depont,	J. Johnson,	J. Bevley,
A. Pelkin,	A. Rhone,	D. Willis,
T. M'Nut,	P. Read,	H. Pelton,
S. M'Carty,	W. Bryant,	W. Moss,
3—Hunts',	D. Cotton,	2—Baleys',
T. Parker,	S. Roberson,	L. Duncan,
J. Sims,	M. Bluren,	G. Mury,
S. Muret,	R. Miller,	G. Pase,
C. Henderson,	T. Ray,	2—Deris',

Transientiers, who travel from place to place.

2—Hains',	L. Taylor,	S. Cooper,
2—Jones',	G. Boalton.	Sparkes,
R. Haris,	3—Levits',	P. Doddridge,

G. Hunter,	H. Helley,	G. Tucker,
C. Moris,	S. Skerlock,	3—Rinins',
Soril Phelps.		

When the above catalogue was finished, Murel observed, "There is not paper to make a proper list, but when you come up to my house we will have time to make a complete one, and this will do until then, as you will not travel any until you go with me a few trips, and learn the routes; and there is not near all the names on this list: but there is no more paper to write on. Hues, I want you to be with me at New Orleans, on the night that the negroes commence their ravages. I intend to head the company that attacks that city myself. I feel an ambition to demolish the city which was defended from the ravages of the British army, by the great General Jackson."

Murel and Hues arrived at Wesley, where they were to part.— Hues promised Murel that he would be ready to see him by three weeks or sooner. They took their leave of each other and parted.

So soon as Murel was out of sight, Hues turned round, and came back to Wesley, and remained there until Murel had time to be several miles ahead. Hues then took another route for Madison county, and made it so as to travel the last ten miles after night, so he might pass without the knowledge of any, only such as he was willing should see him. Hues arrived at Mr. Henning's after midnight, and acquainted his old friend with his adventure, and Murel's confessions concerning his negroes. Mr. Henning collected some of the best citizens of the county, to assist in arresting Murel, a man who had become a pest and terror to the country.

The next night after Hues arrived at Mr. Henning's, the guard was prepared, and they went out after Murel with as much interest as if they were going to rid the country of a thousand hostile savages. Hues was one of the guard, and he requested all the guard to still call him by his assumed name. After Murel was arrested, the officer asked him who went with him to Arkansaw. Murel replied, "a young man by the name of Hues." The officer then asked him if he had ever seen the young man, before he went to Arkansaw.— Murel replied, that he had never seen the young man before he saw him at the bridge at Estanauley, where he got in his company. The officer then called Hues out from the company, into the presence of Murel. When Hues presented himself before him, Murel for the first time, as often as he had been arrested, lost his spirits and fortitude. He appeared as though he would faint, and they gave him water several times before he recovered.

It was the thought of having told so many of the black deeds of his life, and exposed his clan to a man whom he then saw was his enemy, and one of the armed guard to conduct him to justice, that griped the soul of Murel. He saw himself captured and out-generaled by the youth whom he but one moment before, thought lost by the splendor of his horrid crimes, and won by the glittering trappings of infamous gain. These were the thoughts which wrung the flinty heart of Murel, and made his soul sicken at the prospect before him.

Hues was anxious that Murel should not be arrested, until he carried the negroes to Mr. Irvin, and take him in that act; but the citzens were determined to secure him, while they could lay their hands on him. As the guard were taking Murel to the committing court, he enquired of one of the guard who this man Hues was, and whether he had many acquaintances in the country or not. The guard being anxious to hear Murel's ideas, told him that Hues was a stranger. "Well," said Murel, "he had better remained a stranger: I have friends. I had much rather be in my condition than in his." The guard arrived at Jackson with Murel, and he was taken into a tavern, and guarded until a court could be formed. While they were in the tavern, many persons came in to see Murel and Hues; and Hues being willing that Murel should then be undeceived in his name, met his friends as they came in, who called him by the name of Stewart, his real name. Murel now saw that he had been deceived in the name as well as the character of Mr. Stewart, and he saw that Mr. Stewart was universally known by all who entered the room. His spirits, which had a little revived at the idea of his man Hues being a stranger, now began to sink into a double dejection. Murel, though a mystic chief, was caught in a mystery he could not unfold.

Murel was committed to prison in February, 1834, and his trial was to be in the July following.

CHAPTER VI.

The efforts of John A. Murel and his friends for the destruction of the life and character of Mr. Virgil A. Stewart.

After Murel was secure, Mr. Stewart and one of Mr. Henning's sons took a trip through the Yazoo country, in search of Mr. Henning's negroes, as Murel had said that they would go to that market, if they could get through the Choctaw pass or bayou. Mr. Stewart was in hopes of intercepting the boat on the river, before the robbers left it, with the negroes; but on enquiring, boats could not go through the bayou at that time; so they had gone to some other market. Mr. Stewart was very desirous that the negroes should be found, as all the evidence depended on himself; and he neglected his own business, which demanded his presence, to go in search of the negroes.

Mr. Stewart had been trading among the Indians and new settlers of the Choctaw Purchase for about nine months, and intended to settle himself in that country, and had given his name to some of his friends as a candidate for county clerk, before he left there to visit his friends in Tennessee. The election came on while Mr. Stewart was engaged in trying to find the negroes which Murel had stole from Mr. Henning. He passed through the Choctaw Purchase, while making his searches for the negroes, and his friends wanted him to stop and attend to the election : as it was a new country, and but few persons acquainted with each other, candidates were required to mix with the people for an acquaintance ; but Mr. Stewart told his friends that if he was to neglect the business he was then on to electioneer, that he would not deserve an office, or the confidence of community.

After an unsuccessful search, Mr. Stewart returned to Tennessee. Murel's friends were exerting themselves to screen their prince from the penitentiary ; and by this time they were all acquainted with the fact that Murel had given a list of their names to Mr. Stewart, and many of them had stood fair in society, and they were desperately pestered. In short terms, all the land and boon of mystics were in trouble, a spy had visited their camps, and had broke their golden bowl, and carried off captive their chief. So there was weeping among the professors of villainy. There were but two alternatives : they must either destroy the character of Mr. Stewart, or he would destroy them. Mr. Stewart's life would save their chief from the penitentiary ; but that would not restore the lost character of those whom he had disclosed on ; it would only fix their guilt, sealed with his blood, unless they could disgrace him, with dishonor, which would discredit his word.

They soon had several charges, and preferments, afloat against Mr. Stewart, but they all soon disproved themselves, or were confuted by him.

Mr. Stewart returned to the Choctaw Purchase, to prepare some buildings, to settle himself in business. Mr. Stewart had left several trunks of property with a man by the name of Vess, to take care of while he was gone to Tennessee ; but he remained in Tennessee rather longer than what he had expected ; and there being several rumors in the country, that men were seen passing through the country enquiring for Mr. Stewart, bearing arms, and rather suspicious characters, Vess and his wife began to be in hopes that Mr. Stewart was actually murdered, as he had no relations in that country, and left several hundred dollars worth of property in their care, which they intended to hold by fraud; and began to speak of administering on Mr. Stewart's estate, and said that they held a considerable account against him.

They had become so certain of his death, that they began to pick his locks, to examine the contents which they considered as already won ; and among the rest, they examined a purse of silver that they found in one of the chests they opened; they found it containing fifty dollars, but left it with only forty-one: nine dollars sticking fast to their fingers.

When Mr. Stewart came home, Vess and his wife were desperately confused. They calculated that Mr. Stewart would hear of their saying that they held an account against him, which they knew was false; and they knew that Mr. Stewart would miss his silver out of his chest. When Mr. Stewart began to unlock his chests, Vess and his wife looked very wild and confused; and when he missed his money, he asked them if they had opened his chest?— They both denied opening his chest; but said that Mr. Clanton had opened it. Mr. Stewart knew that Mr. Clanton's keys would unlock his locks, and that Mr. Clanton was in the habit of opening his chests and trunks, whenever he wanted any thing that was in them, as they were very intimate, and lived nearly as one family; but Mr. Stewart did not believe that Mr. Clanton had taken his money.— Mr. Stewart concluded to say nothing about his money, as it would hurt the feelings of Mr. Clanton, as he was in the habit of opening his locks; and Mr. Stewart was satisfied how his money went: but he was determined to quit boarding with Vess, so soon as he could get another boarding house.

Several weeks had passed off, and Mr. Stewart had still got no other place to board. When one evening he staid out until after supper was over, so they put supper by for him until he came in; after he had drank one cup of coffee he was taken violently sick, and commenced vomiting. Mr. Stewart was then suspicious that he had drank a dose of poison. Mr. Stewart rode out the next day to look at a tract of land: and in the evening as he was returning home, he was overtaken by a man who had a holster of pistols before him. Mr. Stewart was naturally on his guard against all strangers; and his friends had cautioned him very much to be on his watch, and to go armed, as they calculated, from the threats which had been made, that the friends of Murel would endeavor to kill Mr. Stewart, to dispense with his evidence against Murel; but Mr. Stewart was not armed on that evening, which was a very uncommon thing with him when he rode out. The man who had overtaken him, enquired if he was acquainted in the country about Troy, and began to make several enquiries about the people of that country, and among others he enquired for a family of the Glens, whom Stewart knew to be of Murel's clan; Stewart began to suspect him, and put himself on his guard. The stranger asked Stewart if he was acquainted with a man in that country by the name of V. A. Stewart. When the following dialogue ensued.

"*Mr. Stewart.* Yes, sir, just as well as I would wish to be with all such fellows.

Stranger. What, do you not like him! sir?

Mr. S. I have seen people I like as well.

S. Have you any particular objection to this fellow, Stewart?

Mr. S. O ! yes, many.

S. If you have no objection to telling your objections to this fellow, Stewart, I should like to hear them, as I dislike him very much myself.

Mr. S. O ! he is too smart. Interferes with things which do not concern him. He had no right to take the advantage he did of a man by the name of Murel.

S. Do you understand this ? [giving his hand a flirt. Mr. S. answered the sign with the flirt of the hand] O ! yes, you are up to it. I am glad to see you sir, what is your name ? [shaking hands.]

Mr. S. I have several names ; but whenever I wish to be very smart, or successful in speculation and trade, I go by the name of Tom Goodin. I discover that you are a master of mystic signs—what is your name, sir ?

S. My name is George Aker, sir ! and am on a mission from our council to stop the wind of that d——d Stewart. Can you give me any assistance in that matter ?

Goodin. O ! yes, sir, I am the very man to assist you in that matter. I did not know that there had been a meeting on the subject ; but so soon as I heard of the misfortune, and heard where Stewart lived, I was soon in his neighborhood waiting for a good opportunity. I have been very cautious and still. I have managed to get acquainted with Stewart, and have had some tolerable good chances ; but have been waiting for a better. He thinks me a very clever fellow and I have been waiting to get him off by ourselves.

Aker. We collected and consulted on what plan to pursue to destroy that d——d rascal, and restore the character of those whom he has disclosed on. We have got him in a d——d close box. He is living with his enemies, and the friends of some of the men whom he has disclosed on. We will give him hell before we quit him ; our plan is to get Murel out of prison, and let him go off until court, and after he is gone from prison, get a charge against Stewart, that will destroy his character before the world, and when court comes on Murel will appear for trial, which will convince the world that he is innocent of the charge ; and should Stewart even appear, no person will believe him, for we will prove him to be one of d——est rascals that lives. Murel will be acquitted, and the character of those who have been disclosed on will be restored ; but we never intend for Stewart to live until court, we will kill him and disgrace him too. We have it all fixed—the fellow with whom he lives is a good friend to some of our clan, and we have agreed to give him one thousand dollars to raise a charge against Stewart ; and he is a big fish, and things he says will be believed ; you know we have some big Bugs among us. I am told that he is a confidential friend of Stewart's, and that they have done business for each other. You know that it will be an easy matter for him to make a plausible accusation ; but he will not agree to make the charge against Stewart, until after he is killed as they have always been very friendly, and he wants no investigation by the young tartar. We sent one fellow before, who engaged with an old man and his wife to poison him, for one hundred dollars; but they have not done it from some cause, and we are tired of waiting on them, so they made up two hundred dollars for me, and sent me to despatch the d——d traitor; and if I can get no chance at him this time, before I leave the purchase, we intend to bring men from Arkansaw, with an accusation against him for passing counterfeit money to them ; and in this way get the d——d traitor into our power, and when we get him back into the Mississippi morass we will give him hell ; we will give him something to do besides acting the spy. We will speechify him next time : but I am told that Stewart has managed to get a company to take up strangers who come into the neighborhood after his scalp.

G. Yes, but his company will not be in our way, for I know all his customs, where he walks, and where he sleeps, just as well as he does, and I am not the least suspected by any person, so you know that I can fix him.

A. O ! yes, I count him mine now ; and I will give you one hundred dollars to help me get his scalp. I have no doubt, but the company that went on to get out Murel, has got him out more than a week ago. Where do you live Goodin.

G. I am a little like a stray dog, sir, I have neither home nor master, and stay longest where there are the best speculations to be had ; though I stay mostly in the neighborhood of Commerce at present, and sometimes work to prevent being suspected. I play off occasionally. The people think me a good sort of a fellow, only a little wild. I have still been looking out for every chance that might offer for this fellow Stewart ; I have a choice scatter gun, and one fine pistol, which I keep for the purpose of saving his scalp ; I want it very much. Have you ever been in this country before ?

A. O ! yes ; frequently, though I have not been much seen. I generally come into the neighborhood of an evening, and leave it the next morning before daylight, which you know is the usual mode of visiting among mystics. I had a chance to have seen that d——d curse some time back, at an election at Troy, but there was another fellow who had undertaken to despatch him then, so I let the opportunity pass without improving it. I have never heard the Glens speak of you in this country ; did you not know that they were speculators ?

G. O ! yes, but I never go among them. You know that it is necessary to have some respectable fellows ; and you know that it would not do for me to be among them, as they are suspected, if I wish to play the deep game ; and to be more certain of victory I have never made myself known to any of the Glens, or any of the speculators of this country. If you examine the list you will find my name. I have been looking out for Stewart. We have as much right to play tricks as they have ; but I dislike to run too great a risk for his scalp ; I would like to have a good chance ; and you know there is getting away to be thought of.

A. Do you think you can kill Stewart to-night, and meet me to-morrow at Glen's, to let me hear the news ? you are acquainted in the settlement and are not suspected ; but I am a stranger, and I had rather not be seen by any but my friends, as this company might catch me.

G. I will meet you in the morning, on the path which leads from Glen's to Commerce, at a pile of house logs. Glen can tell you how to go; but you must not let any person come with you in the morning, or say any thing to Glen, or any person else about what is going on. We are enough to know it, as it will be a very daring act. I will act for the best.

A. I will be at the place soon in the morning. Here is one hundred dollars. That is not all you will get, if you are successful in stopping the d——d villain's wind. You say you have a good scatter gun. If you can get no other chance, shoot him as he sits by the fire ; you can get off without being seen, and we will make our escape to Arkansaw together. We can do nothing until he is killed, as we can get no clew at his character until then.

G. That will be a daring project ; but I enter into it with a de-termined mind ; and I am of opinion that you had better not go to Glen's but go with me to a respectable house of my acquaintance, where we will go to bed, and in the night I will get my gun and go to where Stewart boards, and do what I can for him and return to bed before day ; and I have a friend whom I wish to go with us to Arkansaw. We can then leave his house the next morning, and I and my friend can leave the neighborhood without being suspected for the crime.

A. I have some particular business with Glen, relative to some instructions ; and they must be left with him, as he will have the best opportunity of forwarding matters. You go to your acquaint-ance's and do as you have said ; but I had rather not be seen by any but my friends, as a stranger would be suspected much sooner than you. I will go to Glen's, but I will not mention your name to a liv-ing soul, as you are playing the same sort of game upon him that he played upon us. We will keep it all to ourselves, until all is over, and that d——d villain is finished, as you have never made yourself known to the other speculators of this country. Your plan is a good one, and the best of it is to have him beat in his own way.

Aker and Goodin having arrived at the place of separation, Aker remarked :—"Well Goodin, I wish you great success. We meet in the morning at the appointed place." They parted apparently un-der fellow feeling and sentiments.

Mr. Stewart began to reflect on the dangerous condition he was in ; he saw himself surrounded by enemies who were plotting against his life. He was then satisfied that he had drank a dose of poison the night before, and had just parted with a murderous vil-

8

lain, who was an agent to destroy his life. He reflected on the prospect before him in a deep melancholy, and thought of the devoted friendship which he had borne to Clanton, and his interest, and then reflected on the fell treatment which he was receiving, with the deepest regret. He returned home, but instead of going to his boarding house for his supper, he walked over to a Mr. Sander's, an old gentleman of an amiable disposition, with whom he had spent many of his spare hours; after he had taken supper with Mr. Sanders, he went to his boarding house; Mrs. Vess set supper for him, but he refused to take any, telling her that he had supped; she insisted very much on his drinking a cup of coffee, but he refused. He walked out and got under a cart bed which was leaning against the house, where he could watch the manœuvres, and listen to the conversation of Vess and his wife. The coffee which was intended for him to drink, was carried to the door and thrown out; when he saw that, his blood began to boil with revenge.

Mr. Stewart was on the road the next morning by sunrise, with his gun, to meet his intended murderer; he reached the appointed pile of logs, but no Aker appeared. Mr. Stewart waited for Aker until ten o'clock but he never appeared: Mr. Stewart concluded that Aker had, by some means, learned his mistake from his friends and disappeared.

Mr. Stewart has never left any thing, from which a conclusion could be drawn, as to the manner he intended to treat the infamous villain who had engaged him to destroy his own life, more than he went to the appointed place of meeting well armed. Stewart certainly saved his life by the ingenious deception he practised on that rapacious assassin, for had he told his real name, he would have been shot in an instant; for he had no arms to make any defence, while Aker was well armed; and there is no doubt but a sense of his perilous situation sharpened his wits, and prompted him to resort to the ingenious stratagem he practised, when, if he had been armed, he would have pursued a different course; but the kind protection of Providence was guarding the safety of Stewart, and let man learn from the history of this transaction the protection of Heaven.

Stewart returned home in trouble and disquietude; he had commenced building to settle himself, and was anxious to commence business; but he saw it would not do for him to settle at that place where he was surrounded with his enemies.

He concluded to finish the house which he had commenced, and then leave the country until after the trial of John A. Murel, so as to evade the operations of his enemies. He was troubled to think that Mr. Matthew Clanton could be hired to do him an injury, or that he would take sides with such infamous villains. He studied on it for several days, and sometimes he would reproach himself for believing that Clanton could be hired for so base a purpose; and then he would recollect that Clanton would never join the company which was formed to keep those suspicious characters out of the neighborhood; which was very important to his safety. Stewart intended to move his boarding to Mr. Sanders', so soon as he could. He never would eat at Vess' any more, only when all were eating together, and he tried them several nights; when supper would be prepared for just himself, the coffee was always thrown out after he walked out of the house.

A few days had passed off very dull with Mr. Stewart, when one morning he received a letter from a friend in Tennessee, which informed him of John A. Murel's escape from prison. This intelligence revived all that had passed with him and George Aker, and seemed to be a warning to leave the dangerous place which he then occupied.

Before Mr. Stewart had left the purchase, to visit his friends in Tennessee at the time he was solicited to follow John A. Murel, he had taken the care of Matthew Clanton's business for about six weeks, until Clanton could go into Tennessee after his family, as Clanton had no clerk, and wanted to go after his family, Stewart consented to attend to his business until he returned: although his own business suffered for the want of his attention during the time; Clanton and Stewart had been very friendly from their first acquaintance, and they had been acquainted with each other over in Tennessee, before they moved into the Purchase; and Stewart is one of those kind of young men who will neglect his own business, to befriend or oblige a friend. He is entirely devoted in matters of friendship. Clanton's business was a rough concern, with but little regularity in the way it was managed; it consisted of remnants, and old goods, and such things as could be sold to the Indians, and new settlers of that country. He had a day book in which he set down the running accounts of those whom he credited, and a ledger in which they were posted, and a drawer in the writing desk, in which he put all the cash that was received for goods, or any thing which was sold, but no cash book, and when an article was sold for cash, the money was deposited in the drawer, and no further notice was taken of it. Stewart raised but one new account on Clanton's books while he attended to his business, and that was against himself, for a man by the name of Smith; that is, the goods were for Smith; but Stewart assumed the payment of the debt as he was owing Smith on a running account for corn. The two accounts were open, and whenever Smith wanted an article from the store it was charged, and when Stewart wanted corn he got it from Smith. Stewart could have paid Smith the money for his corn, just as easily as he could pay Clanton for his goods; but he bartered with Smith to throw the money into the hands of Clanton: whom he believed to be his friend. So when Stewart wanted any thing from the store himself, he paid the money into the drawer, as he had one running account on the books for Smith. During the six weeks, Stewart had got five or six dollars worth of articles for himself, and took in more than ninety dollars from others, for spirits and different articles. This amount was thrown into the drawer in one common pile, as it was received by littles ; but when a regular customer paid his account on the book, the receipt of the amount was entered under the account.

Clanton returned home and received his business from the hands of Stewart, and was highly pleased with the way Stewart had managed his business during his absence. Stewart settled the account he had raised for Smith with Clanton, and paid over all the money which he had collected, and what he had received for goods sold.— Clanton was so pleased with the way Stewart had attended to his business during his absence, that he complimented him with a lot in a little place which he had laid off for a town ; but he had not been offered a large bribe at that time, to traduce the character of Stewart, or perhaps we would then have heard a different story from Clanton, as to the honor of Stewart. Though at that time Stewart had not interfered with the proceedings of villains : no mystic lords had then been exposed by Stewart, whose fate depended on his destruction. Clanton then had no inducements to act dishonest ; and he could then believe Stewart an honorable young man.

Stewart having acquitted himself of Clanton's business, he left the Purchase for Tennessee, in January 1834, on private business, where he was solicited by his friend, Mr. Henning, to follow John A. Murel, and try to regain his negroes which had been stolen from his possession.

Stewart quit Clanton's business in January 1834, and the May following Clanton took exceptions to the way Stewart had managed his business, by charging him with dishonor, and said that he had not paid for the goods which he had got for himself from the store, while he had attended to his business. This accusation was made by Clanton, about one month after Stewart had returned home from Tennessee, and the second day after he had heard that John A. Murel had made his escape from prison. The only reason that Clanton could advance for his accusation against Stewart was, that he had not made an account of the articles which he had got for himself, instead of paying for them : recollect that Stewart had one running account on the books for Smith, and he did not wish to have a complexed account, for that reason he paid for the articles which he got for himself. Stewart is not acquainted with the rules and customs of clerks, neither did he consider himself Clanton's clerk ; he considered himself his agent, and attended to all his business as an agent. Stewart could see no difference in paying for an article, and using it himself, or selling it to another man ; and there is no difference with an honest man. Clanton could, with equal propriety, demanded an account of every article which was sold for cash by Stewart, which is contrary to his mode of doing business ; for Clanton used no cash book in his establishment. If Clanton was honest in his accusation against Stewart's honor, why this delay of five months before he made his accusation ? He had time to examine his business before he received it from the hands of Stewart, and after Stewart was gone to Tennessee, Clanton opened his trunks and chests whenever he wanted any of his tools, instruments, books or any thing he had; this was a liberty that Stewart allowed him, and thought it nothing more than a mark of confiding friendship; and we see Stewart loosing nine dollars from his chest, and saying nothing about it, because Clanton was in the habit of unlocking it; this he done to save the feelings of Clanton, because he believed Clanton to be an honest man: and he believed that Vess and his wife had taken his money from the chest; and would then put Clanton under censure to save themselves. Clanton had every opportunity to examine the articles which Stewart had got from his store for four months; and if he believed that Stewart had not paid for them, why would he wait until May before he disclosed it? The reason why Clanton delayed his accusation until so late a period was, he had not been offered a bribe of one thousand dollars to traduce the character of Stewart until then: and so soon as this was the case, his imagination was very fertile in framing accusations against the honor of Stewart.

When Clanton made his accusation against Stewart, he affected to be sorry, and whenever he spoke of it, he dissembled regret:— this was his stratagem to give effect to his base accusation. Yes, he could have wept over Stewart and shed a flood of crocodile tears for a few dollars. Stewart was then convinced that Clanton was the man whom George Aker had alluded to, for the matter had then been fairly demonstrated by the charge made. Stewart returned the town lot which he had been complimented with by Clanton; and told him that he would not receive any thing from the hands of a man who would charge him with dishonor. Stewart was advised by a friend, (whose experience enabled him to discover the base treatment he was receiving.) to settle his business in the Purchase, and go out of the influence and power of his enemies.— Stewart knowing that his life was in danger so long as he remained where he was, concluded to go to Lexington, Kentucky, and prepare the publication of John A. Murel's confessions and plans against community, together with their plans against his life and character. The former he considered due to his country, and the latter due to himself and friends. He selected Lexington, because he had private business at that place, and he considered that he would be as secure from the operations of his enemies in that city, as any other. In a few days Stewart had his business so arranged that he could leave it: and when he was prepared to start, he told Clanton that whenever he was convinced that he had acted dishonorable towards him, to publish it to the world; but cautioned him of the bad consequences of being too premature in his conclusions and engagements. Stewart left the Purchase for Lexington, Kentucky: he passed through his old neighborhood in Tennessee, and spent a few days with his friends, and the community for whom he had risked so much, and enthralled himself in so many dangers and difficulties; and incurred the never dying hatred of a host of spirits, who are more wicked and revengeful than the Prince of Darkness; but Stewart looked on his labors as lost, and himself injured, for Murel had escaped from prison, and left him nothing for his dangerous adventures only the information which Murel had given. Stewart was no company for his friends, neither were there enjoyments in those objects around him with which he was once delighted: he is one of those noble spirited youths who regards his honor and character as being all that are worth living for, and the least infringement on either is calculated to render him unhappy; and he saw himself surrounded with a legion of devils and slanderers, whose fate depended on his destruction. Their plan of operation he had learned from one of their clan, and that they were operating, he could have no doubts; under such reflections as these, there were nothing but the thunders of slander continually roaring in his ears: their designs against his life had become a small matter with him, when compared with their designs for the destruction of his character.

In a short time after Stewart had left the Purchase, Clanton and his agents had it circulated over the country, that Stewart had stolen a quantity of goods from Clanton and run away. Such reports were very mortifying to the feelings of Stewart; and he started on to Lexington to prepare the publication, which he had designed for the public, so soon as the trial of John A. Murel was over; but now that Murel had made his escape from prison before his trial, he deemed it his duty to lay before the world all the confessions and plans of John A. Murel and his clan against community; and here we are led to pay a tribute of respect to the nobleness of heart, and magnanimous feelings of Stewart; and even to a man whom he knew to be of the basest and most corrupt principles; and agreeable to the confessions of his own tongue, his hands were often dyed in the blood of his fellow-beings. Yet we see Stewart withholding the horrid confessions, designs, and life of Murel, as given by himself, from even his best friends, and divulging nothing on Murel before his trial, only what was connected in some way with the crime for which he was then prosecuted, that he might have a fair trial, before legal representatives of his country, for the crime he was then to answer for. This Stewart done, that the minds of the people might not be prejudiced to unreasonableness against Murel, until after his trial, that law and justice might be administered.

A short time after Stewart left his friends in Tennessee, for Lexington, John A. Murel was re-taken in Alabama, as was supposed, directing the operations of his plans; and as Stewart was the only evidence on the part of the State, he was immediately followed by a young gentleman, to inform him of the re-capture of Murel.— Stewart returned to Madison county, and waited until Murel's trial, which took place in July, 1834. After Murel was taken, his friends were the more industrious in trying to traduce the character of

Stewart, and they were disappointed in their favorite plan of getting
Stewart into their power, by the false accusation of having passed
counterfeit money to them in Arkansaw.   When Clanton first made
his accusation against Stewart, it was done to excite suspicion in
the minds of Stewart's friends in the Purchase, so as to enable his
accusers from Arkansaw to carry him off to Arkansaw, to answer
to their accusations against him; where they intended to torture
him to death.   Stewart had many warm friends in the Purchase,
whose confidence it was necessary to shake before their designs
could have been effected, and that was their stratagem to accomplish it; and we have other corresponding evidence which agrees
with the assertions of George Aker in that matter—which is a copy
of a letter that was found in the possession of John A. Murel, by
the Sheriff of Madison county, some short time after he was re-taken.*   This letter directed certain individuals of his clan how to
proceed with their accusation from Arkansaw, against Stewart, but
they were disappointed in their fiendish purposes, and Murel again
in the iron grasp of the law, before their bloody designs against
Stewart could be accomplished, and the time of trial drawing near,
their hopes were all hung on the accusation which Clanton had
made against Stewart's honor:—and Matthew Clanton and his
agents began to discover, that all who were acquainted with Stewart looked on his accusation with contempt, so they saw the neces-
sity of supporting his charge with more substantial reasons, and
enlarging it.   Stewart had been keeping house for several years before he moved to the Choctaw Purchase, and when he started to
move, he packed up all his china-ware, and table furniture in a chest,
and carried it with him, as he expected to need it at some future
day.   All these things Clanton accused Stewart of getting from his
store, notwithstanding they had been used for several years.   This
he done to make his charge of as much consequence as possible, by
reporting that Stewart had fitted himself out for house keeping from
his store, and had not accounted for it on the books; but as Providence would have it, Stewart was among his old neighbors, who
knew that he had kept house, and some of them had assisted him in
packing up his furniture to move, so the enlargement upon the accusation was equally disrespected with the first.   Stewart was very
secluded after he returned to Madison county, until after the trial of
John A. Murel was over, and his mind was alive to all the marvellous
and strange circumstances which had attended him in his adventure, from the commencement.   He was led to believe, that he was
directed and protected by a superior power, whose guardian protection took up and unfolded every plan which was laid for his destruction, and defeated his enemies in all their designs against him.—

* This letter was read in court as evidence against Murel, and is filed in the Clerk's
office in Madison county.   This copy of the letter was retained by Murel to preserve
uniformity in their conduct.   I have no copy of the letter, or it would have been giv-
en in this for publication.

Stewart was never heard to express a harsh sentiment against
Clanton, until he heard the enlargement of his accusation, as he was
not fully satisfied on the subject until then, as he did not know what
management had been employed by Vess and his wife to effect their
designs with Clanton, for he looked on these two people as he would
on two fiends of hell, who were prepared to commit the most horrid crimes that the imagination is capable of conceiving; although
other circumstances were conclusive against Clanton, yet Stewart
was loath to relinquish him, and whenever he spoke of Clanton, it
was with allowance : and would observe, that he not only deserved
Clanton's confidence, but that he deserved his eternal respect ; but
when Stewart heard that Clanton had included all his furniture
which he had been using for several years, his resentment was as
obvious as Clanton's guilt was apparent, for that was a matter in
which Clanton could not be misled, unless he wished to be. Stewart is one of those young men who is devoted in his friendship, gen-
erous in his sentiments, and true to his country ; and where he has
once felt a particular respect; his friendship is almost implacable.—
Stewart was too well known, for their base machinations to effect
his testimony ; and too many had proved the honor of Stewart to
believe that he was worth no more than five dollars, or that he would
treat Clanton with injustice.

The trial of John A. Murel came on, and the court house was
crowded to overflowing, with the deeply anxious spectators, who
crowded around to hear the mystic web of Murel's daring feats of
villainy unravelled before the jury that were to decide this important
case, in which the community were so deeply interested. The witness, Virgil A. Stewart, was called—he appeared before the court
and waiting congregation, and was sworn :—he then commenced
his evidence, by giving a narrative of his adventure, and developing
all the circumstances and occurrences which led to the introduction
and acquaintance with Murel and himself—frequently giving the
subject of their conversation, and the language of the prisoner, as
he expressed himself when in the company of the witness, and all
those feats of villainy, denominated and distinguished by the prisoner as the feats of this elder brother ; together with the manner in
which the prisoner made himself known to the witness, as being this
elder brother himself. He gave the occurrences and subjects of
conversation, as connected with the confessions of the prisoner,
both before and after he made himself known as the elder brother ;
and the wonderful actor of those feats which he had related.

The witness commenced his testimony in the afternoon, and was
stopped at dark, and the next morning resumed his place before the
court and finished the evidence. He was many hours engaged in
making disclosures, and was then cross-examined by the prisoner's
counsel, on the evidence he had given in on the preceding day. His
answers were clear and satisfactory to all but the prisoner and his
friends. The manner of Murel's detection, having disclosed on his

friends, they were afraid to appear in court, for fear of being known, and dealt with as such; this misfortune of Murel's had disarmed him; for had it not been for that, he could have proved any thing that he wanted by his own clan; but now that their names were on a list which were given to the witness by Murel himself, they would not dare to venture into court to his assistance.

Murel and his clan, failing to destroy the evidence of Stewart, they endeavored to prove that he was interested in the conviction of Murel, and that Parson Henning had hired him to detect John A. Murel, and got a man by the name of Reuben McVey, who was an enemy to Stewart, to come into court and swear, that Stewart had told him the fact; but he, like all other liars, was caught in his own net, not Stewart; his story had so many contradictions in it, that it was no evidence. Stewart was prepared to prove that Mc-Vey had sworn to a lie; but the prosecuting counsel considered his evidence had proved itself to be a lie. So far from Stewart being hired to undergo the danger which he has done, in this adventure, he would not even receive a present of a handsome suit of clothes which Parson Henning wished to purchase for him; as he had spent more than a month in riding after his negroes. Parson Henning was anxious to make Stewart a handsome present, as a token of his gratitude, for the kindness of Stewart; but he would not accept it.

A specimen of malignant hatred. McVey ruins himself, by trying to do Stewart an injury. Stewart never considered McVey a man of honor, and for that reason he would not associate with him, which was the spleen.

Stewart's evidence was supported by the first class of gentlemen that the country afforded.

John A. Murel was found guilty of negro stealing and sentenced to the penitentiary for ten years at hard labor.

During the pleadings, a Mr. Brown, one of Murel's lawyers bore on the feelings of Stewart in an unwarrantable and dishonorable manner, for which Stewart was determined to give him a Stansberry reproof, so soon as he could meet him on the Street; but he was prevented by his friends, who were old men, and he felt himself bound to respect their advice and request. Thus ended the trial and conviction of the great Western Land Pirate, who had reduced villainy to a system, and steeled his heart against all of the human family, except those who will consent to be as vile as himself.

9

CHAPTER VII.

Some time after the trial of John A. Murel, Stewart left Madison county, for Lexington, Kentucky, with the intention of preparing the publication of the life, confessions, and designs of Murel and his clan against community, together with their base and horrid efforts, and designs, which had been made and employed against his life, and character; which duty he considered due to his country and himself; and which he was determined to perform, notwithstanding the dangerous consequences attending it were fairly presented to him, in all the most hideous forms of danger and horror which the imagination is capable of conceiving, by the private agents of the clan, who came in the garb of friends to Stewart. All such stratagems as these have been employed with Stewart, to deter him from publishing to the world, their black and horrid deeds, awful designs, and unnatural purposes. Yet we see Stewart moving on with a firm nerve, to the performance of what he conceived to be his duty, undaunted by all the fictions of horror and death, which they were capable of presenting to his imagination.

As Stewart was going on to Lexington, he turned off from the main road, and went into Perry county, to see a gentleman who had written to him concerning purchasing a tract of land which Stewart owned, in the State of Mississippi: as it was not much out of his way, and he had been advised by his friends to go a circuitous route, to evade any efforts of his enemies that might be attempted, by following or intercepting him on the way. Stewart attended to his business in Perry county, and intended to cross Tennessee river above Perryville, and to go by the way of Columbia and Nashville; but the determined perpetrators of crime and iniquity were too eager to glut their never dying vengeance, by imbruing their hands in the blood of Stewart, (and they calculated to gain the possession of those hated documents, which had caused them so much unhappiness and disquietude, with their victory over Stewart, which would greatly enrich their conquest; and double the value of their prize, as it would not only destroy the repugnant cause, but it would erase the more dreaded and heated effect, by preventing a publication to which they felt such an aversion,) to suffer him to leave the country without their knowledge, notwithstanding his precaution in not letting the time be known to even his best friends, until he was prepared to start. Stewart had got on one of those long stretches, where there were no houses for several miles, on the road leading from Jackson to Patton's ferry on Tennessee river, in a broken hilly country; as he was descending one of those hills, he was suddenly stopped by three armed men, who had been concealed behind trees until he had arrived within a few rods of them. The man on his right ordered him to dismount from his horse, but Stewart refused, notwithstanding the superior number and arms which he saw around him, whose hostile vengeance were depicted in every countenance, as they stood with the instruments of death grasped in the willing hand, and expected every moment to feel the fatal messenger of death, with his chilling power, cooling the warm fluids of life which flowed in his heart. He saw himself in the very jaws of death; but the grim monster did not unarm the firm and resolute Stewart; he was determined to sell his life as dear as possible, and die defending the sacred gift, which he had received from his creator; or at least to avoid the awful and cruel death of torture, which he knew the fiends, who had him in their power, would gladly inflict—and sport around the hideous altar with gay derision, glorying in the sacrifice they were offering to their Mystic Deity. Stewart was armed with nothing but a small pistol, which he had not more than two hours before taken from his portmanteau, and placed in his side pocket for convenience; and a good strong dagger which he carried in his bosom. The assassin on his right, who was within about two rods of Stewart, was armed with a large fowling piece, and the man on his left was armed with a good looking rifle, and the monster who stood by a tree, which was nearest the road, placing him nearly in front, but at some distance before, was armed with a horseman's pistol. Thus displayed, forming a triangle, into which Stewart had entered. The assassin on his right appeared to be the commander, and after he had ordered Stewart to dismount several times, and still advancing until he was within eight or nine feet of him, he then halted and asked Stewart if he intended to dismount from his horse—to which inquiry he gave a negative answer. The assassin commenced levelling his piece on him, but Stewart being very expert in the use of a pistol, fired at the assassin's face, the ball struck him on the corner of his forehead, he fell back, apparently lifeless, and as he fell, his gun fired, but the muzzle had dropped nearly to the ground, and the contents struck the earth just after it passed under the belly of Stewart's horse. The assassin who was posted on his left, presented his rifle and fired without effect. The assassin who was stationed in front, with the horseman's pistol, seeing that Stewart had drawn no other pistol, only the one which he had fired, concluded that Stewart was then unarmed, so he, to make a sure shot, advanced within a few feet of Stewart, and levelled his pistol at his breast; but just as he was bearing on the trigger, Stewart threw his empty pistol, with all his power, at the face of the assassin, and struck him over one eye, and across the nose—the assassin's pistol snapped, and fell from his hand. He spurred forward his horse, and made several strokes at the assassin; but he could not get near enough to him for the full force of his strokes to be received by the assassin:—while he was engaged in trying to kill this fellow with his dagger, the other assassin, who had the rifle, gave him two blows with his heavy rifle—the last blow was received on the back part of the neck, just where the head and neck joins, which came very near unjointing his neck, though it did not disengage him from his horse. He found that he was badly wounded, and betook himself to flight: and after he had gone thirty or forty yards from the scene of action, the horseman's pistol was fired at him; one shot passed slightly through his left arm. Stewart had got about 3 miles from where he had received his wound, when he was compelled to dismount from his horse from exerutiating pain. He selected a thick wood, in a dale, under the brow of a steep hill, for a stopping place, as he hoped that its friendly protection would obscure him from the view of the merciless assassins; as he was then too far exhausted to contend any longer for his life. He remained in this wood until the next day, being unable to leave it. He had frequent fits of delirium during the night, and the next morning he began to reflect on his unhappy condition, and perhaps not in possession of his proper mind from his resolutions. He reflected on the dangers which surrounded him, until he came to the conclusion that it was his duty to leave America. His mind being fixed on its purpose of departure, he directed his course for Columbus, in the State of Mississippi. His sufferings were great; but he still travelled until he reached near the centre of the Chickasaw nation, where he was compelled to stop travelling for several days. He lay at the hut of an old Indian who treated him with great kindness. He continued his journey to Columbus as soon as he was able to ride, where he intended to take water for Mobile, at which city he intended to leave his documents and papers, in the hands of a friend, to prepare for the press; but he was disappointed in getting a boat for Mobile.— So he concluded to take water from some point on the Mississippi river, but he was taken down before his journey was completed, with a return of the inflammatory effects of the wound in his head. And his travelling so long before he would give up, greatly augmented the severe pain which he endured, but he was compelled to yield the giant resolutions of the mind to the weakness of a wounded and fainting body, that appeared to be relaxing its power for a dissolution; his fits of delirium became alarming, and he began to consider his recovery as very uncertain; and made such arrangements as he wished, concerning himself and his affairs. By his request, I had engaged to perform his wishes, and take charge of all his business and papers.

Stewart is recovering his health and mind, both of which have been greatly injured.

BIOGRAPHICAL SKETCH OF

MR. VIRGIL A. STEWART.

He was born in Jackson county, in the State of Georgia, of respectable parentage, and was remarked for his steady habits while
very young—a young man who is governed by high and honorable
motives—of liberal and independent sentiments—honorable and
correct in his dealings—grateful to his friends, and has many pecul-
iar traits or character. He is hated and dreaded by all villains—respected and esteemed in every country where he has lived, by its
best citizens.

The following declarations of sentiments are given for the satisfaction of those who are disposed to enquire into his merits.

STATE OF GEORGIA—Jackson county.

The undersigned, citizens of said State and county, do certify,
that we have been acquainted with Mr. Virgil A. Stewart, former-
ly of this county, now of Madison county, and State of Tennessee,
for a number of years, (and some of us from his infancy) and that
he has always supported a respectable and honorable character, and
we take pleasure in recommending him to the confidence of the citizens of whatsoever county he may visit, assuring them that we entertain no fears, of his ever doing any act derogatory to his character as an American citizen, or in the least calculated to forfeit the
confidence, to which he is herein recommended. Given under our
hands, 15th Feb. A. D. 1833.

Wm. E. Jones, L. L. D. Giles Mitchell, L. L. D. George R.
Grant, M. D. David Witt, Esq. Middleton Witt, L. L. D. H. Hemp-
hill, John Appleby, George F. Adams, James D. Smith, Loyd W.
Shackelford, E. C. Shackelford, Augustus J. Brown, Esq. William
Cowan, Green R. Duke, L. A. K. Lowry, Wm. E. Davis, John
Mackelnanon, John Carmicheal, Wm. N. Wood, Charles Bason,
John Lindsley, Samuel Watson, Wm. H. Jones, Wm. Morgan,
Jackson Bell, James Cunningham, Mr. D. A. C. Bacon, Lewis
Chandler, Wm. Niblock, G. M. Lester, John Park, Maj. William
Park, Samuel Barnet, Col. J. W. Glen, Esq. John Shackelford,
James Nabers, James Orr, George Shaw, Maj. Wm. D. Martin,
Esq. Charles Witt.

GEORGIA—Jackson county.

I, Sylvanus Ripley, Clerk of the Superior and Inferior Courts of
said county, do hereby certify that I am acquainted with Mr. Stewart, the person named in the above recommendation, and believe

him to be of good moral character; and also with the persons whose names are signed to the same, as professionally connected, who are entitled to the same.

Given under my hand and seal of office, the 27th day of February, A. D. 1833.

SYLVANUS RIPLEY, Clerk. [L. s.]

GEORGIA—Jackson county.

I, Edward Adams, one of the Judges, and Chairman of the Inferior Court for the county aforesaid, do hereby certify, that Sylvanus Ripley, who gave the above certificate, is the Clerk of said Courts, and that his acts as such are entitled to all due faith and credit, and I further certify, that I am well acquainted with Mr. Virgil A. Stewart, and heartily accord with the sentiments expressed by the above respectable citizens of this county.

Given under my hand and seal of office, the 27th day of February, A. D. 1833.

EDWARD ADAMS, J. I. C. [L. s.]

STATE OF TENNESSEE—Madison county.

The undersigned, citizens of said State and county, do certify that we have been acquainted with Mr. Virgil A. Stewart, ever since he emigrated from the State of Georgia to this country, and that he has supported a character of firmness and unsullied honor.

Given under our hands, the 15th day of March, A. D. 1833.

John Henning, William Long, Byrd Hill, Thomas Loftin, Wm. Evens, Mathias Boon, John Givens, R. H. Byrn.

The following is the declaration of sentiments expressed by the citizens of Madison county, and community, towards Mr. Virgil A. Stewart, for his intrepidity in ferreting out the conduct, and capturing John A. Murel, the great Western Land Pirate.

STATE OF TENNESSEE—Madison county.

We, the undersigned, citizens of said State and county, feeling sensibly the obligation which we are under to Mr. Virgil A. Stewart, for the many dangers which he has encountered with courage and intrepidity, in ferreting out the Land Pirate, John A. Murel, and bringing him to justice, present the amount annexed to our names

71

as a donation, and token of our gratitude, for the important and dangerous services rendered by Mr. Stewart, in capturing said Pirate: believing, as we do, that he is entitled to it, for the loss of time and expenses which were necessarily incurred by Mr. Stewart for the public good:—and we mean further: by this subscription and declaration of sentiment, to manifest to the world our approbation and applause, for the course pursued by Mr. Stewart, and not only appreciate his courage, but discountenance the odium which has been attempted at his character, in pursuing so disagreeable a course for the good of community—and we further consider, that he deserves to be protected and upheld, by all society, in the course he has pursued.

William Armour, Allen Deberry, A. Petton, B. W. Burrow, M. Chalmers, Labon Dodson, M. Deberry, M. Cartmel, Jacob Hill, William Taylor, C. T. Harris, James Voss, Gabriel Anderson, John Garrison, D. D. McDonald, B. W. Perry, Samuel Givens, F. C. Edwards, E. H. Childers, Samuel Hays, J. H. Rawlings, Mills Durdin, Thomas Campbell, R. H. Lake, Hazael Hewett, H. R. Lacy, John Sanford, Zebulon Jackson, G. Slayton, Alfred Sharp, S. Sypert, George Hicks, John Harrison, John Burrow, F. McKenzie, E. McKnight, A. Hutchens, G. Snider, John T. Porter, Philip Worlick, Mathias Boon, Thomas H. Shores, H. S. Ross.

I, Mathias Deberry, do hereby certify, that I am, and have been, the Sheriff of the county aforesaid, for a number of years, and that I am personally acquainted with all the persons whose names appear to the above declaration of sentiments, and take pleasure in testifying, to all whom it may concern, that they are of the most honorable and respectable class of citizens of our State; and that the above declaration of sentiments towards Mr. Stewart, has been subscribed to by all the like characters who have had an opportunity presented, as far as I have reason to believe; and that the above subscription was unsolicited on the part of Mr. Stewart.

Given under my hand, at Jackson, the 29th day of September, A. D. 1834.

MATHIAS DEBERRY, Sheriff.

The following is the copy of a letter, written by Mr. Virgil A. Stewart, to one of his friends, in which we are enabled to discover many traits of his character and disposition.

MADISON COUNTY, Sept. 15. 1834.

Dear Sir—I received your kind letter of the 10th. I am truly grateful for the many tokens of friendship which you have manifested towards me, and your advice, which your age and experience would compel me to respect, exclusively of the deep interest which, I have every reason to believe, you have long felt in my welfare

and happiness. You manifested some fears that I would endeavor
to avenge myself on the person of Matthew Clanton ; but be assured, sir, that I have no such intentions ; notwithstanding I consider
he deserves my greatest abhorrence, yet I had much rather he should
live to enjoy the tortures of a reproaching conscience, and the
rich infamy for which he bartered his principles, than to stain my
hands and character with his blood. Vengeance belongs to our
Creator alone, under whose guardian protection I look for ample
support in that matter. I will unfold his infamous conduct, and present things to the world as they are, and let an enlightened world
judge between me and Matthew Clanton. So long as I was doubt-
ful on the point of his being misled by others, I framed as many ex-
cuses for him as I could, and examined all my conduct, to see if it
was calculated in the least to excite suspicion. I was also cautious
of speaking derogatory of his character ; for so long as I could have
had the least shadow of belief that Matthew Clanton was honest in
his charge against me, and that any imprudent conduct in me had
been calculated to excite his suspicion of my honor, I would sooner
have sought refuge from the unjust reproach of the world, among
the savage haunts of the forest, where the track of civilized man
has never yet been made, than to have uttered one word that would
have been the least calculated to injure his character. Yes, sir, I
had rather spend my days among savage haunts, where there is no
sound but that of beasts of prey and savage yells to be heard, with
peace of conscience, than to enjoy all the plaudits and honors of
an admiring world, with the bitter reflection, that my enjoyment
had cost the destruction of the happiness or character of one innocent fellow-being. Be assured, sir, that I will never resort to violence and rashness, unless it is provoked, and I could resort to such
a course only while in the heat of a passion, which I shall never encourage. I will endeavor to be governed by more laudible principles.

I feel the truest pleasure in seeing and knowing that my friends
and community, resent the dishonorable treatment I received from
Mr. Brown, in his sophistical pleadings. And I would here remark,
that the assumed privilege of abuse and calumny, and sarcasm on
witnesses (when supported in it by good evidence,) by the gentleman of the bar, is calculated, in the highest degree, to retard the operation of law and justice—and if all men were of my opinion on
that subject, it would be relinquished by them, only when supported
by unquestionable evidence.

I wish to remind you of the unfair propositions, or rather syllogisms in the sallies of his pleading :

1st. He declared that I had acted with deception, and practised a
falsehood on John A. Murel, in procuring his confidence, by representing myself as a horse hunter, and a villain : and contended that
he who will act a falsehood or practice a deception, will, or the next

step is to swear to it;—and therefore I deserve no credit—and should not be credited, or respected by a human being, &c.

2d. He represented me as the friend of John A. Murel, and declared, that a man who would betray the confidence of his confiding friend was a villain, and that I had betrayed the confidence of my confiding friend, therefore I was a villain, &c.

To the above dishonorable and unfair mode of reasoning, (in a court of justice at least,) I thus reply to Mr. Brown. When I went after John A. Murel, I was not after a friend, but an enemy to me, and all honest community, whose outrages were insufferable ; and whose systematical plans evaded all attempts of the law to bring him to justice. Thus lay the insulted dignity of our national institutions, which were erected and established for the protection of our lives, liberty and property, trampled under foot of that daring incendiary and his practical legion, who gloried in the carnage they were making in our property ; and the disquietude they produced in the social hands of society, having for their end the destruction of both the former and the latter. In my opposition to this formidable banditti, I honestly considered that I was authorized to imitate the acts of our great men of the nation, as the biography of great men are given as a pattern and guide for the youth of the rising generations, and to which I am indebted for the most of my little knowledge of man, and the physical world :—and whose opinions and acts, we are bound to respect in proportion to the renown of the actor.

As to the deceptions I practised on John A. Murel, in obtaining his confidence and disclosures, I refer you to the following in justification of my acts.

Recollect the deception practised by Gen. Washington (at the time Major Andre, the British spy, was captured,) in trying to get Arnold, the traitor, back into his possession ; and recollect Washington's reasonings on that subject. Sir, they will sustain me, and cover Mr. Brown with shame and confusion. And again I refer you to the deception of Col. Washington, at Claremont. See his stratagem, in causing the garrison to surrender by a deception he practiced upon them, in mounting the trunk of a pine tree on wagon wheels, so as to resemble a field piece, which caused them to surrender ; and has ever been considered a gallant act of Col. Washington. But because I dissembled the character of a villain, for the purpose of learning the conduct of many villains, and ridding a community of a craft that is destructive to the peace and happiness of all civil and honest society, Mr. Brown is not willing that I should ever wear any other character only the infamous one which I represented to John A. Murel ; and he professed to see no virtuous motives in my conduct which propelled me to action. No, Sir, as there were no large fees or some other selfish consideration to influence my actions it was a mysterious matter with him, because his own narrow soul is too small to render the same services;—and for that very reason, all such men as Milton Brown have no right to express their

10

contracted views of me and my conduct :—and if expressed, entitled to no credit. I consider him, and all such men, nothing more than the organ through which the venom of a detestable and piratical clan of villains was vented towards me, whose machinations and calumny were ignobly piled on my character by Mr. Brown, like another ignominious hireling in iniquity.

Would Mr. Brown condemn the deceptions of either of the Mr. Washington's, as above related ; if he would not, he must sustain me, for the deceptions as above related, and mine with John A. Murel, are synonomous in principle, both having the same object in view, and would be the same at the bar of moral rectitude; only the acts of the former are the acts of illustrious persons, and the latter the acts of an obscure young man.

I entered into no oaths with John A. Murel and his clan, neither have I forfeited any promises. I complied with the only promise which I made to John A. Murel, which was to visit him within three weeks or sooner from the time I parted with him at Wesley, which promise I complied with, or fulfilled in a few nights after we parted, for I visited him in company with the guard on the night that he was arrested, which visit saves my promise. Neither did I make any assertions of deception for which I ever expect to receive the disapprobation of my Creator. Yet Mr. Brown asserted that I had lied to serve my country, and that the next step was to swear to a lie—and will he say that General Washington lied to serve his country, and that the next step he would have sworn to a lie for the sake of getting the traitor Arnold into his power, because he resorted to a stratagem, to restore justice to his injured country. Sir, there is nothing more detestable to me than a vain sceptic.

As to betraying the confidence of a friend, I consider that I have at least as much honor as Milton Brown, and I hope more love for my country, and less vanity for self aggrandizement—I feel the greatest contempt for Mr. Brown's calumny, and no man who cherishes correct principles could have so wantonly and so uncalled for, heaped abuse on the character of a man who had underwent the dangers and disagreeable trials which I was necessarily compelled to undergo, in capturing John A. Murel ; and what makes his scepticism and abuse the more disgusting to good sense and feeling, it was unsupported with even the shadow of evidence, and must have flowed from a desire to please a train of villains, and a piratical clan of robbers, together with the hope of acquiring the character of a great criminal lawyer, without the least regard for truth, honor, justice or principle.

It is the duty of a lawyer to see that his client has been legally dealt with, and that if he is convicted, he is convicted agreeable to law ; but he has no right to abuse the character of a witness, when he has no proof to sustain his abuse, merely because he is a witness. Sir, I do contend, that it was my duty to cane Mr. Brown, to teach him a lesson which he ought to learn, although I was governed in that by the advice of my best friends. My evidence was supported by the best of characters, and there was no exceptions taken to my evidence, on the cross examination, and why that volley of abuse which I received from that son of vanity? Mr. Brown resorted to barefaced lying in his pleadings. Recollect that part of my evidence where Murel turned off from the road to eat; you know that I stated to the jury, that I asked Murel his reasons for going so far from the road to eat? he replied that he would not be surprised if that d——d old Methodist, whom he had been telling me of, was to have some person following him, knowing him to be a particular friend of those two young men of Madison county; and that, if there was any person following him, he would much rather have them before him than behind him; as he would know better how to manage them. Therefore he went into the woods to eat, so as not to be seen by passengers who might pass while we were eating; but mark the way that Mr. Brown tried to turn that part of my evidence in his pleadings. He contended, that I said that Murel told me to go on, that he had much rather have people who were following him, before than behind him. By this barefaced perversion of my evidence, he tried to prove that Murel knew that I was the man who was following him; and as such, would not have made so many disclosures to me. Look at his shallow scheme: how could Murel say to me, go on, when he was before me, and me following him—and when Mr. Brown was corrected by the Judge, he still contended obstinately that he was correct.

Sir, please to indulge a few syllogisms of mine. Any attorney who will wantonly lie, and misrepresent evidence, for the sake of getting an opportunity to abuse a witness, to please a clan of villains, or heap calumny and abuse on a witness when he is supported in it by evidedce, for the sake of acquiring the character of a great criminal lawyer, is a base, corrupt, and dishonorable man; and should not be respected by a human being. Milton Brown has done all these things. Therefore he is a base, corrupt, and dishonorable man, and should not be respected by a human being on earth.

I am determined never to let any thing that is said of me, by mean men, render me the least unhappy. If I can escape violent hands, that is as much as I can reasonably look for, placed in my disagreeable situation; I have every reason to believe, that the honest world are all my friends; and I have every evidence of their respect, which I shall forever endeavor to deserve. I expect to start to Lexington in a few days.

With great and sincere esteem, I am
Your most obedient friend and servant,
VIRGIL A. STEWART.

The above letter is given, because it developes the views and sentiments of Mr. Stewart, relative to his course of conduct with Murel and his friends, much better than we are able to describe them.

Titles available from

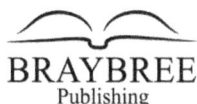

BRAYBREE
Publishing

A Sacred High Place: A History of Mount Carmel Cemetery and Meetinghouse, McNairy County, Tennessee
by John E. Talbott, J.D. • ISBN 978-0-9671251-9-0

A History of Dickson County, Tennessee
by Dr. Robert E. Corlew • ISBN 978-1-940127-00-2

Gold is the Key: Murder, Robbery, & the Gold Rush in Jackson, Tennessee
by Thomas L. Aud • ISBN 978-0-9671251-3-8

The Peg Leg Politician: Adam Huntsman of Tennessee
by Kevin D. McCann • ISBN 978-0-9671251-4-5

The Jackson Generals: Minor League Baseball in Jackson, Tennessee
by Kevin D. McCann • ISBN 978-0-9671251-7-6

Hurst's Wurst: Colonel Fielding Hurst & the Sixth Tennessee Cavalry U.S.A.
by Kevin D. McCann • ISBN 978-0-9671251-2-1